GRADE 3 PHONICS AND SPELLING

TABLE OF CONTENTS

1. UNIT 1 Consonant & Vowels - PAGE 1
2. UNIT 2 Beginning, Middle and Ending Consonant Sounds - PAGE 7
3. UNIT 3 Short Vowels - PAGE 14
4. UNIT 4 Long Vowel A - PAGE 21
5. UNIT 5 Long Vowel E - PAGE 24
6. UNIT 6 Long Vowel I - PAGE 27
7. UNIT 7 Long Vowel O - PAGE 34
8. UNIT 8 Long Vowel U - PAGE 37
9. UNIT 9 Syllables - PAGE 44
10. UNIT 10 Syllables - PAGE 51
11. UNIT 11 Y As Long Vowel E & I - PAGE 58
12. UNIT 12 Hard and Soft C & G - PAGE 65
13. UNIT 13 R Blends - PAGE 72
14. UNIT 14 L Blends - PAGE 79
15. UNIT 15 S Blends - PAGE 86
16. UNIT 16 Final Consonant Blends - PAGE 93
17. UNIT 17 R-Controlled Vowels AR & OR - PAGE 100
18. UNIT 18 R-Controlled Vowels ER, IR & UR - PAGE 107
19. UNIT 19 Compound Words - PAGE 114
20. UNIT 20 Diphthongs Oi, Oy, Ou, Ow - PAGE 121
21. UNIT 21 Diphthongs Au, Aw, Ew, Oo - PAGE 128
22. UNIT 22 Vowel Pairs Ai, Ea, Ie, Oa, Ue - PAGE 135
23. UNIT 23 Digraphs CH, SH, WH, TH - PAGE 142
24. UNIT 24 Digraphs PH, GH, KN, GN - PAGE 149
25. UNIT 25 Silent Letters WR & MB - PAGE 156

Grade 3 Phonics and Spelling Workbook   *Created by Mrs. Indira Coleby-Demeritte*

UNIT 1 Consonant & Vowels   Page 1

MONDAY — PHONICS PRACTICE

Color all of the **vowels red** and the **consonants yellow** on each mango.

a b c d e f g h
i j k l m n
o p q r s t
u v w x y z

TUESDAY — PHONICS PRACTICE

Count the amount of consonants in each word and write the number in the box.

book	☐	hat	☐
car	☐	mom	☐
desk	☐	dress	☐
pencil	☐	clock	☐

Grade 3 Phonics and Spelling Workbook   Created by Mrs. Indira Coleby-Demeritte

UNIT 1 Consonant & Vowels — Page 2

WEDNESDAY — PHONICS PRACTICE

Circle the missing vowel or consonant for each word.

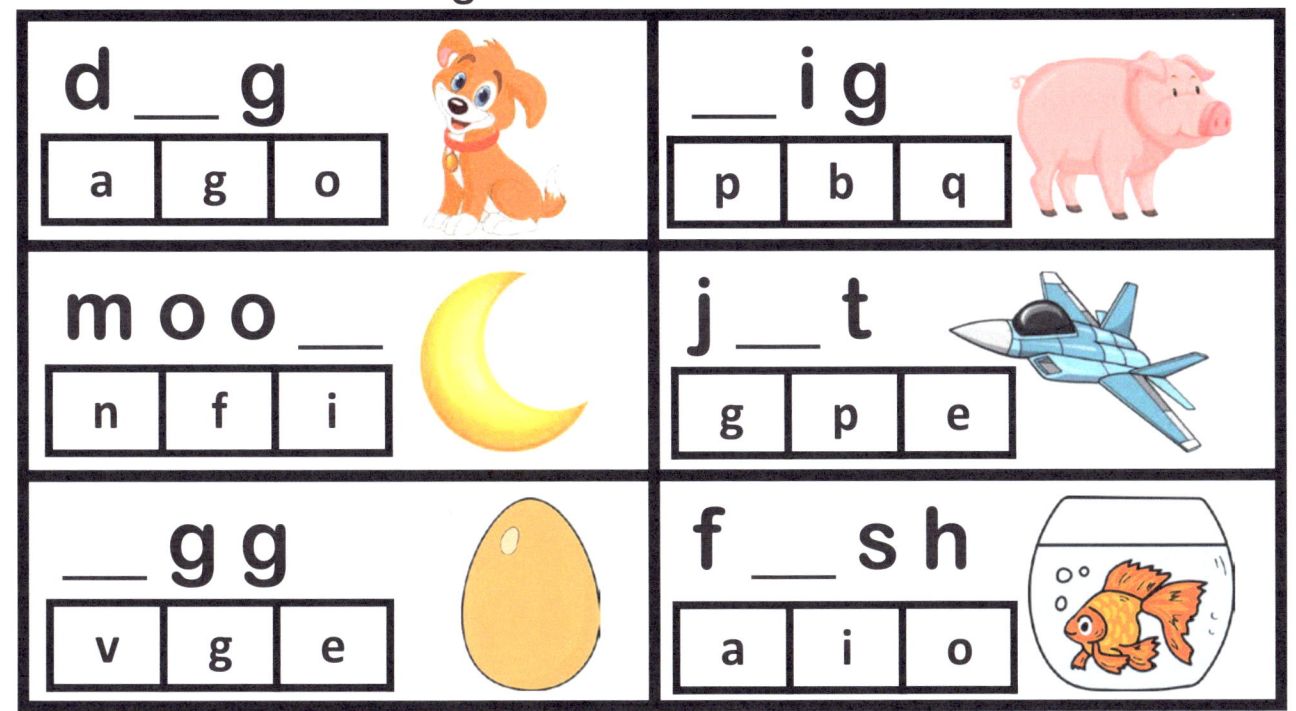

d __ g	a g o
__ i g	p b q
m o o __	n f i
j __ t	g p e
__ g g	v g e
f __ s h	a i o

THURSDAY — PHONICS PRACTICE

Sort the letters below into vowels and consonants. Write them in their group.

q	t	o	d	j
w	y	p	f	k
e	u	a	g	l
r	i	s	h	m

VOWELS

CONSONANTS

Grade 3 Phonics and Spelling Workbook — Created by Mrs. Indira Coleby-Demeritte

UNIT 1 Consonant & Vowels Page 3

ASSESSMENT

Date: _____   Score: _____

Use the letters on the buttons to sort the vowels and consonants on the tablet.

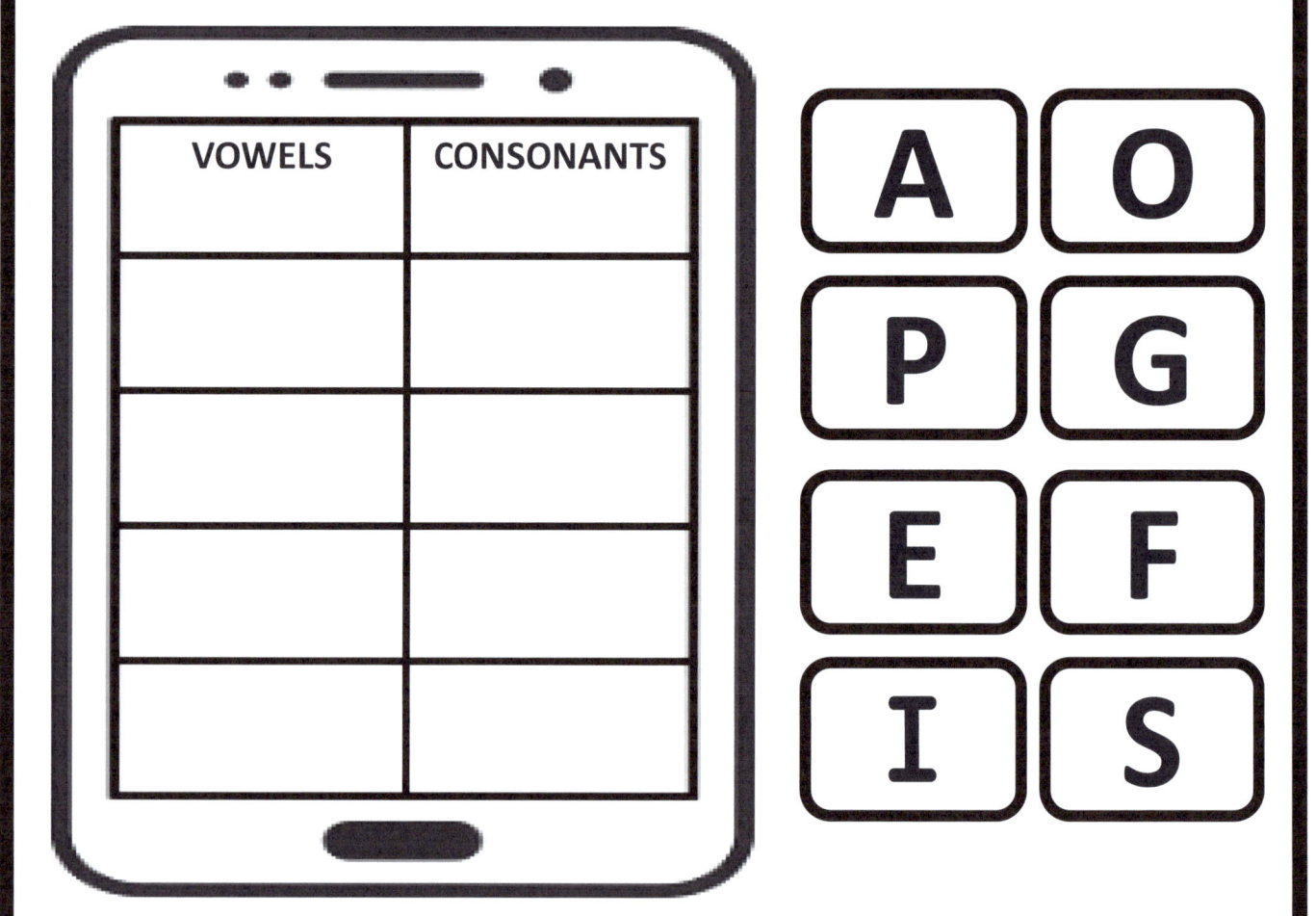

VOWELS	CONSONANTS

Buttons: A, O, P, G, E, F, I, S

Look at each word then count the vowels you see and write the number in the box.

tree ☐	rose ☐
net ☐	brown ☐

Grade 3 Phonics and Spelling Workbook   *Created by Mrs. Indira Coleby-Demeritte*

UNIT 1 Consonant & Vowels

Page 4

MONDAY — SPELLING PRACTICE

Use your spelling list to write the word for each picture.

(purple circle) _____	(math) _____
20 _____	(reading) _____
(science) _____	(red circle) ___

TUESDAY — SPELLING PRACTICE

Unscramble the spelling words. The first letter is underlined.

eidn<u>r</u>ag _____

hat<u>m</u> _____

lyu<u>J</u> _____

ndrdu<u>h</u>e _____

gust<u>A</u>u _____

<u>T</u>dyause _____

de<u>r</u> _____

cneic<u>s</u>e _____

Spelling Words

reading
purple
math
science
Tuesday
twenty
July
hundred
red
August

Grade 3 Phonics and Spelling Workbook — Created by Mrs. Indira Coleby-Demeritte

UNIT 1 Consonant & Vowels — Page 5

WEDNESDAY — SPELLING PRACTICE

Use your spelling list to sort the spelling words. Some words may be used on both groups.

Words with T	Words with A

THURSDAY — SPELLING PRACTICE

Fill the letters in the blank to complete each word.

R __ a d __ __ g
P u __ p __ __
M __ __ h
__ w e __ t __
__ u g u __ t
S __ __ e __ c e
H __ n d __ __ d
__ u e s __ a y

Spelling Words

1. reading
2. purple
3. math
4. science
5. Tuesday
6. twenty
7. July
8. hundred
9. red
10. August

Grade 3 Phonics and Spelling Workbook — Created by Mrs. Indira Coleby-Demeritte

UNIT 1 Consonant & Vowels — Page 6

Practice the spelling of each word below by writing it in its column.

reading	purple	math	science	Tuesday

twenty	July	hundred	red	August

Grade 3 Phonics and Spelling Workbook — Created by Mrs. Indira Coleby-Demeritte

UNIT 2 Beginning, Middle and Ending Consonant Sounds — Page 7

MONDAY — PHONICS PRACTICE

Say each picture name. Circle the letter that stands for each beginning sound.

m c b	p j l	p t v
d s m	w r z	k f y
z d r	d v s	b z j

TUESDAY — PHONICS PRACTICE

Say the name of each picture. Write the letter that stands for the middle sound.

Le __ on	Sha __ ow	Ti __ er
Ca __ in	Pa __ er	Mo __ ey

Grade 3 Phonics and Spelling Workbook — Created by Mrs. Indira Coleby-Demeritte

UNIT 2 Beginning, Middle and Ending Consonant Sounds — Page 8

WEDNESDAY — PHONICS PRACTICE

Say the name of the picture in the first box. Color the pictures in the row that end with the same sound.

THURSDAY — PHONICS PRACTICE

Write the word that makes each sentence tell about the picture.

| puppy | daddy | bubbles | kitten | ladder |

- I watched some _____ fly up high.
- A _____ ran into the garden.
- My _____ climbed up onto a branch.
- I shouted for my _____ to get my cat.

Grade 3 Phonics and Spelling Workbook — Created by Mrs. Indira Coleby-Demeritte

UNIT 2 Beginning, Middle and Ending Consonant Sounds Page 9

ASSESSMENT

Date: _____   Score: _____

Directions: Name each picture. Listen for the sound at the beginning of each row. If you hear the sound at the beginning of the word, fill in the first bubble. If you hear the sound in the middle of the word, fill in the second bubble. If you hear the sound at the end of the word, fill in the third bubble.

m | 1. | 2. | 3. | 4.

d | 1. | 2. | 3. | 4.

g | 1. | 2. | 3. | 4.

s | 1. | 2. | 3. | 4.

t | 1. | 2. | 3. | 4.

Grade 3 Phonics and Spelling Workbook   *Created by Mrs. Indira Coleby-Demeritte*

UNIT 2 Beginning, Middle and Ending Consonant Sounds **Page 10**

MONDAY — SPELLING PRACTICE

Use your spelling list to write the spelling for the picture.

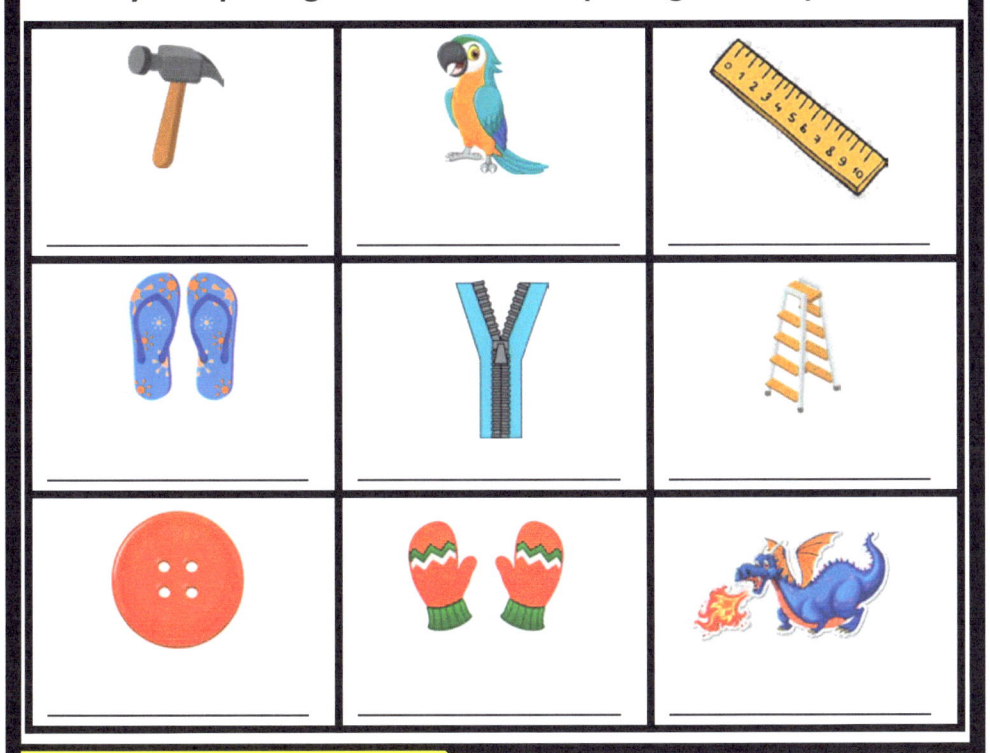

hammer _____	parrot _____	ruler _____
slipper _____	zipper _____	ladder _____
button _____	mitten _____	dragon _____

TUESDAY — SPELLING PRACTICE

Use the word box to write a rhyming word.

sister	kitten	slipper
button	seven	dragon

wagon _____
mister _____
zipper _____
mitten _____
mutton _____
heaven _____

Spelling Words

1. mitten
2. slipper
3. tiger
4. dragon
5. cannot
6. sister
7. zipper
8. seven
9. kitten
10. button
11. forest
12. ladder
13. person
14. lemon
15. parrot
16. hammer
17. ruler
18. balloon
19. bird
20. camel

Grade 3 Phonics and Spelling Workbook *Created by Mrs. Indira Coleby-Demeritte*

UNIT 2 Beginning, Middle and Ending Consonant Sounds — Page 11

WEDNESDAY — SPELLING PRACTICE

Unscramble the spelling words. The first letter is underlined.

1. id<u>b</u>r _____
2. ven<u>s</u>e _____
3. e<u>p</u>snor _____
4. no<u>l</u>em _____
5. mel<u>c</u>a _____
6. ntno<u>c</u>a _____
7. leur<u>r</u> _____
8. <u>d</u>ognra _____
9. ste<u>f</u>or _____
10. get<u>i</u>r _____

THURSDAY — SPELLING PRACTICE

Circle the word that is spelled correctly in each set.

person pirsen purson persin	ballon balon baloon balloon	ladeer lader ladder lauder
rulir ruler ruleer roler	jragon dragon dagon draggon	parot parut parrot paruit

Spelling Words

1. mitten
2. slipper
3. tiger
4. dragon
5. cannot
6. sister
7. zipper
8. seven
9. kitten
10. button
11. forest
12. ladder
13. person
14. lemon
15. parrot
16. hammer
17. ruler
18. balloon
19. bird
20. camel

UNIT 2 Beginning, Middle and Ending Consonant Sounds — Page 12

Practice the spelling of each word below by writing it in it's column.

mitten	cannot	kitten	person	ruler

slipper	sister	button	lemon	balloon

Grade 3 Phonics and Spelling Workbook — Created by Mrs. Indira Coleby-Demeritte

UNIT 2 Beginning, Middle and Ending Consonant Sounds

Practice the spelling of each word below by writing it in it's column.

tiger	zipper	forest	parrot	bird

dragon	seven	ladder	hammer	camel

Grade 3 Phonics and Spelling Workbook   *Created by Mrs. Indira Coleby-Demeritte*

UNIT 3 Short Vowels   Page 14

MONDAY — PHONICS PRACTICE

Look at each picture, say the name of the picture to yourself and write the vowel sound you hear in the box.

lips ☐	bed ☐	lock ☐
bus ☐	ham ☐	car ☐
nest ☐	sun ☐	pin ☐

TUESDAY — PHONICS PRACTICE

Look at each picture, say the name to yourself and then write in the missing vowel to complete the word

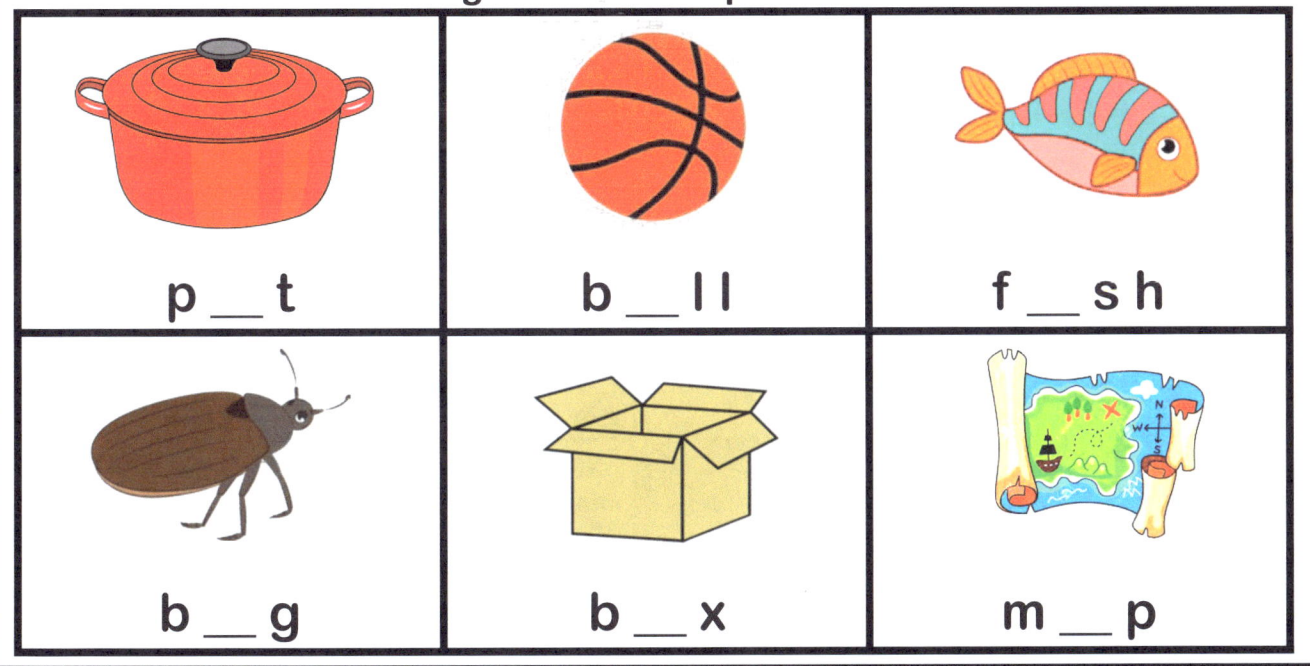

| p __ t | b __ ll | f __ sh |
| b __ g | b __ x | m __ p |

Grade 3 Phonics and Spelling Workbook *Created by Mrs. Indira Coleby-Demeritte*

UNIT 3 Short Vowels

WEDNESDAY — PHONICS PRACTICE

Look at the word bank. Use the words to fill in the blanks. Then read the story!

| got | pot | hot | Bob | cob | top |

Corn on the Cob

_____ was making dinner.
First, he put water in the _____.
Then, he put the pot on _____ of the stove.
Soon the water was _____.
Bob _____ the corn and put it in the pot.
What did Bob eat? Corn on the _____!

THURSDAY — PHONICS PRACTICE

Read the story and answer the questions.

Buck, the Duck

My friend, Buck, is a funny little duck. Instead of quacking, he clucks. Each day, he rides to school in our truck. One day, I asked, "Buck, why do you cluck?" He said, "Well, Chuck, I am speaking another language when I cluck."

1. What is Buck?
   _____

2. How does Buck and his friend get to school?
   _____

3. Why does Buck cluck?
   _____

4. What is the best meaning for language?
   A) communication B) talk C) write D) sign

Circle all of the -uck words in the story and then write the words in the box below.

Grade 3 Phonics and Spelling Workbook — Created by Mrs. Indira Coleby-Demeritte

UNIT 3 Short Vowels   Page 16

ASSESSMENT

Date: _____   Score: _____

Directions: Read each sentence. Circle the word that completes the sentence and write it on the line.

	1. The dog sat in the _____ .	set / sun / sick
	2. The pig is on the _____ .	mop / map / mat
	3. The bug is in the _____ .	top / net / nest
	4. I put him in the _____ .	tub / tan / top
	5. The _____ is in the mud.	cot / cub / can
	6. He can _____ .	dig / den / dot
	7. A fish has a _____ .	fat / fin / fell
	8. The egg came from the _____ .	hen / hot / hip

Grade 3 Phonics and Spelling Workbook   *Created by Mrs. Indira Coleby-Demeritte*

UNIT 3 Short Vowels

Page 17

MONDAY — SPELLING PRACTICE

Fill in the vowel sound you hear for each picture.

cl _ ck	_ mbr _ ll _	gl _ ss
l _ ve	_ ctop _ s	sm _ ll

TUESDAY — SPELLING PRACTICE

Use the word box to write the rhyming word.

| dug | past | under | clock | next |

1. thunder _____
2. last _____
3. rug _____
4. text _____
5. lock _____

Spelling Words

1. little
2. rock
3. past
4. dug
5. next
6. bottom
7. clock
8. under
9. glass
10. hamburger
11. city
12. them
13. love
14. umbrella
15. octopus
16. sticky
17. lunch
18. smell
19. pumpkin
20. astronaut

Grade 3 Phonics and Spelling Workbook   Created by Mrs. Indira Coleby-Demeritte

UNIT 3 Short Vowels Page 18

WEDNESDAY — SPELLING PRACTICE

Unscramble the spelling words. The first letter is underlined.

1. tl_i_tle _____
2. sta_p_ _____
3. mur_g_haebr _____
4. ickt_s_y _____
5. el_s_ml _____
6. ncu_l_h _____
7. um_p_pkin _____
8. tron_a_suat _____
9. t_b_otmo _____
10. larbe_u_ml _____

THURSDAY — SPELLING PRACTICE

Look at the first letter of each word. Write the words in Alphabetical Order. The alphabet chart below will help you. The first one has been done for you.

A B C D **E** F G H **I** J K L M N **O** P Q R S T **U** V W X Y Z

1. bottom
2. little
3. hamburger
4. ~~astronaut~~
5. pumpkin

astronaut

Spelling Words

1. little
2. rock
3. past
4. dug
5. next
6. bottom
7. clock
8. under
9. glass
10. hamburger
11. city
12. them
13. love
14. umbrella
15. octopus
16. sticky
17. lunch
18. smell
19. pumpkin
20. astronaut

Grade 3 Phonics and Spelling Workbook Created by Mrs. Indira Coleby-Demeritte

UNIT 3 Short Vowels

Practice the spelling of each word below by writing it in its column.

little	bottom	city	sticky	rock

clock	them	lunch	past	under

Grade 3 Phonics and Spelling Workbook — *Created by Mrs. Indira Coleby-Demeritte*

UNIT 3 Short Vowels

Practice the spelling of each word below by writing it in it's column.

love	smell	dug	glass	umbrella

pumpkin	next	hamburger	octopus	astronaut

Grade 3 Phonics and Spelling Workbook   *Created by Mrs. Indira Coleby-Demeritte*

UNIT 4 Long Vowel A — Page 21

MONDAY — PHONICS PRACTICE

Write the letters a – e to complete each picture name that has the long a sound.

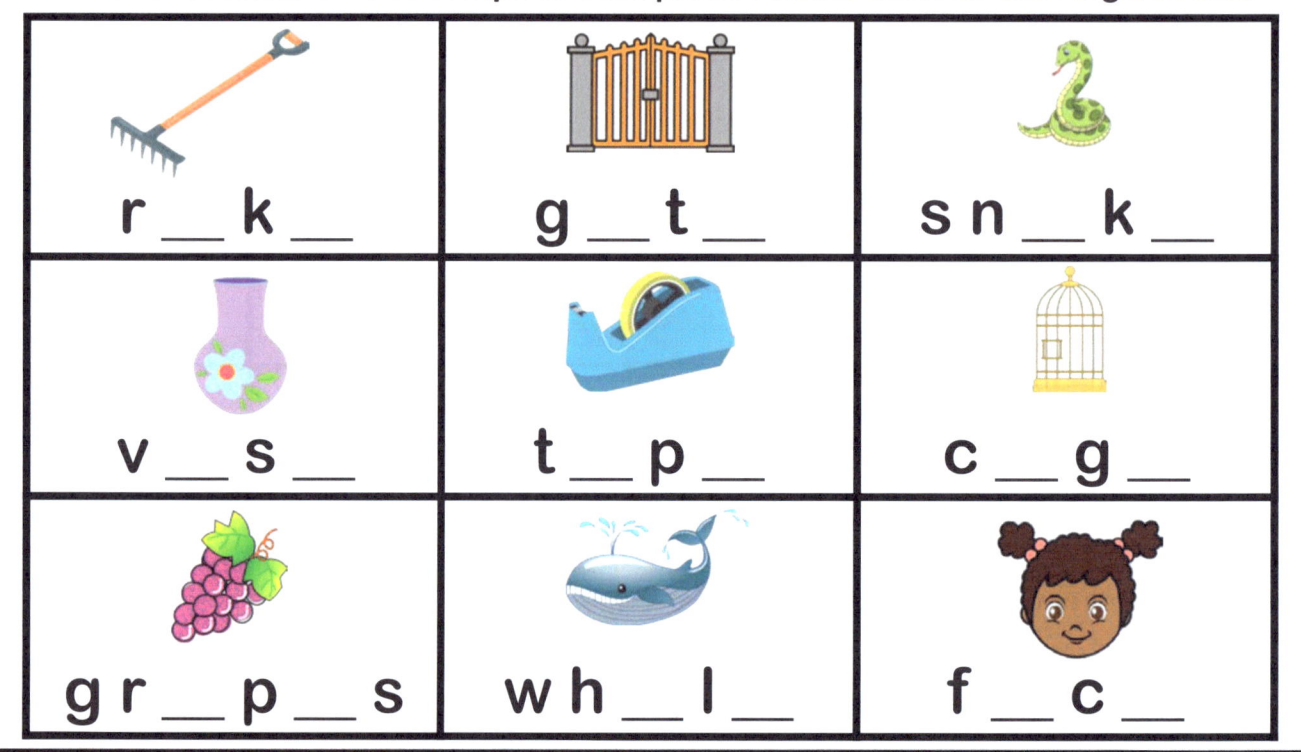

r __ k __	g __ t __	s n __ k __
v __ s __	t __ p __	c __ g __
g r __ p __ s	w h __ l __	f __ c __

TUESDAY — PHONICS PRACTICE

Long Vowel A can be written many ways. It can be written as <u>Ai or Ay</u>. <u>Ai</u> is used mostly in the middle of words. <u>Ay</u> is used mostly at the end of words. Look at the picture below, add ai or ay to complete the spelling of each word.

p __ __ l	p __ __	s p r __ __
h __ __	r __ __ n	c h __ __ n

Grade 3 Phonics and Spelling Workbook — Created by Mrs. Indira Coleby-Demeritte

UNIT 4 Long Vowel A

WEDNESDAY — PHONICS PRACTICE

Look at the word bank. Use the words to fill in the blanks. Then read the story!

| day | play | gray | rain | pail | paint |

Rainy Day

Grandma and I will _____ the porch.
We have our brushes.
We have a _____ of _____ paint.
Then it starts to _____!
"Tomorrow is another _____," says Grandma.
"Let's go inside and _____. "

THURSDAY — PHONICS PRACTICE

Read the story and answer the questions.

Ace, the Ape

Ace, the ape, lived in a cave by the lake. He baked a cake from grapes and dates. One day, Ace put on his skates and twirled around with his cake on a plate. Oops! Ace fell in the lake with his cake.

1. Where did Ace live?
   _____

2. What did Ace, the ape, bake?
   _____

3. What did Ace put on one day?
   _____

4. What is a synonym for date?
   A) veggie B) candy C) fruit D) drink

Circle all of the a __ e words in the story and then write the words in the box below.

Grade 3 Phonics and Spelling Workbook — Created by Mrs. Indira Coleby-Demeritte

UNIT 4 Long Vowel A — Page 23

ASSESSMENT

Date: _____   Score: _____

Directions: Use the words in the box below to complete the sentences. Write the rhyming words.

> gate   rain   rake   tail
> cake   mail   skate   train

1. _____ rhymes with _____

2. _____ rhymes with _____

3. _____ rhymes with _____

4. _____ rhymes with _____

Grade 3 Phonics and Spelling Workbook   *Created by Mrs. Indira Coleby-Demeritte*

UNIT 5 Long Vowel E

Page 24

MONDAY — PHONICS PRACTICE

Say the name of the picture in the first box. Circle the picture whose name rhymes with it.

knee	net	pan	bee
seal	hose	tire	tie
cheese	5	trees	man
sheep	soap	hen	jeep

TUESDAY — PHONICS PRACTICE

The letters ee often stand for the long e sound. Write ee to complete each picture name.

| h __ l | thr __ __ | p __ __ l |
| tr __ __ | sl __ __ p | kn __ __ |

Grade 3 Phonics and Spelling Workbook *Created by Mrs. Indira Coleby-Demeritte*

UNIT 5 Long Vowel E

WEDNESDAY — PHONICS PRACTICE

Look at the word bank. Use the words to fill in the blanks. Then read the story!

| bees | eating | Jean | need | see | sleep |

What Did Jean See?

_____ sat under a big _____.
"I _____ a nap," she said.
But there were so many things to _____!
Jean looked at some ducks _____ grass.
Then she looked at some _____ buzzing around flowers. "I will _____ later," Jean said. "I'd rather look around!"

THURSDAY — PHONICS PRACTICE

Read the story and answer the questions.

Beach Trip

I like to go to the beach. It is always clean. It is neat to hear the wind blow from the ocean. I like to eat ice cream, when I get hot. My parents likes to drink tea, when they get hot. We have a real nice tent to help with shade. It is white and teal. When I get back home, I sometimes dream about the fun summer I had at the beach.

1. Where do I like to go?
_____

2. What do I like to hear from the ocean?
_____

3. What do my parents like to drink when they get hot?
_____

4. What is a synonym for <u>beach</u>?
Ⓐ shore Ⓑ path Ⓒ hill Ⓓ road

Circle all of the <u>ea</u> words in the story and then write the words in the box below.

UNIT 5 Long Vowel E — Page 26

ASSESSMENT

Date: _____   Score: _____

Directions: Say the name for each picture. Write the long "E" word that names the picture. Use the words from the word box to help you.

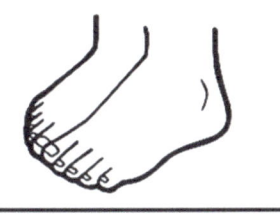

leaf	key	bee	meat
tea	eel	seal	feet

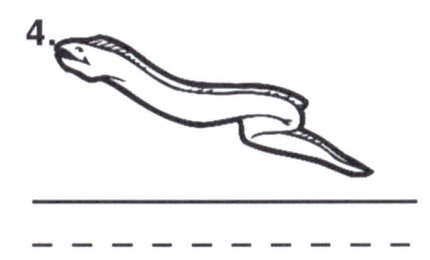

1. _____
2. _____
3. _____
4. _____
5. _____
6. _____
7. _____
8. _____

Grade 3 Phonics and Spelling Workbook   *Created by Mrs. Indira Coleby-Demeritte*

UNIT 6 Long Vowel I   Page 27

MONDAY — PHONICS PRACTICE

Say the name of the picture in the first box. Circle the picture whose name rhymes with it.

TUESDAY — PHONICS PRACTICE

The letters ie often stand for the long i sound. Write ie to complete each picture name.

t _ _ s   p _ _ s   fr _ _ s

cr _ _ d   fl _ _ s   sk _ _ s

Grade 3 Phonics and Spelling Workbook   *Created by Mrs. Indira Coleby-Demeritte*

UNIT 6 Long Vowel I — Page 28

WEDNESDAY — PHONICS PRACTICE

Look at the word bank. Use the words to fill in the blanks. Then read the story!

| hide | ride | five | write | time | slice |

Things I Like

Here are _____ things that I like.
I like to _____ my bike.
I like to eat a _____ of pizza.
I like to _____ my name.
I like to play _____ and seek.
I like to have a good _____ with people I like!

THURSDAY — PHONICS PRACTICE

The letters igh often stand for the long i sound. Write igh to complete each picture name.

n _ _ _ t

l _ _ _ t

f l _ _ _ t

s _ _ _ t

f _ _ _ t

k n _ _ _ t

Grade 3 Phonics and Spelling Workbook   Created by Mrs. Indira Coleby-Demeritte

| UNIT 6 Long Vowel I | Page 29 |

ASSESSMENT

Date: _____   Score: _____

Directions: Read the word on the left. Draw a line to the picture on the right that matches the word.

1. tire
2. bike
3. pie
4. night
5. dime
6. five
7. tie
8. mice

Grade 3 Phonics and Spelling Workbook   *Created by Mrs. Indira Coleby-Demeritte*

UNITS 4-6 Long Vowels A, E & I

Page 30

MONDAY — SPELLING PRACTICE

Use your spelling list to write the spelling for the picture.

(sheep)	 (train)	 (reptiles)
 (spray)	 (teacup)	 (crime)
 (wheel)	 (playground)	 (rice)

TUESDAY — SPELLING PRACTICE

Classify the spelling words into their vowel groups.

LONG VOWEL A	LONG VOWEL E	LONG VOWEL I

Spelling Words

1. teamwork
2. teacup
3. reach
4. sheep
5. breathe
6. concrete
7. wheel
8. crime
9. lifetime
10. wise
11. reptiles
12. rice
13. tried
14. main
15. spray
16. explain
17. playground
18. blame
19. awake
20. train

UNITS 4-6 Long Vowels A, E & I — Page 31

WEDNESDAY — SPELLING PRACTICE

Use the word box to write a rhyming word for the words below.

reach	sheep	wheel	rice
spray	train	blame	awake

1. Same _____
2. Steel _____
3. Pray _____
4. Rain _____
5. Mice _____
6. Beach _____
7. Mistake _____
8. Sleep _____

THURSDAY — SPELLING PRACTICE

Look at the first letter of each word. Write the words in Alphabetical Order. The alphabet chart below will help you.

A B C D E F G H I J K L M N O P Q R S T U V W X Y Z

1. tried
2. awake
3. lifetime
4. concrete
5. explain

Spelling Words

1. teamwork
2. teacup
3. reach
4. sheep
5. breathe
6. concrete
7. wheel
8. crime
9. lifetime
10. wise
11. reptiles
12. rice
13. tried
14. main
15. spray
16. explain
17. playground
18. blame
19. awake
20. train

Grade 3 Phonics and Spelling Workbook — Created by Mrs. Indira Coleby-Demeritte

UNITS 4-6 Long Vowels A, E & I — Page 32

Practice the spelling of each word below by writing it in it's column.

teamwork	concrete	reptiles	explain	teacup

wheel	rice	playground	reach	crime

Grade 3 Phonics and Spelling Workbook — *Created by Mrs. Indira Coleby-Demeritte*

UNITS 4-6 Long Vowels A, E & I — Page 33

Practice the spelling of each word below by writing it in it's column.

tried	blame	sheep	lifetime	main

awake	breathe	wise	spray	train

Grade 3 Phonics and Spelling Workbook — *Created by Mrs. Indira Coleby-Demeritte*

UNIT 7 Long Vowel O

Page 34

MONDAY — PHONICS PRACTICE

Say the name of the picture in the first box. Circle the picture whose name rhymes with it.

TUESDAY — PHONICS PRACTICE

The letters oa often stand for the long o sound. Write oa to complete each picture name.

c _ _ t   r _ _ d   g _ _ t

t _ _ d   c _ _ ch   fl _ _ t

Grade 3 Phonics and Spelling Workbook   *Created by Mrs. Indira Coleby-Demeritte*

UNIT 7 Long Vowel O

Page 35

WEDNESDAY — PHONICS PRACTICE

Look at the word bank. Use the words to fill in the blanks. Then read the story!

| phone | note | home | hope | rose | wrote |

A Note From Rose

_____ went away to camp.
At first, she missed her _____.
She _____ many letters to Mom and Dad.
She also called them on the _____.
Then Rose wasn't homesick anymore!
This is the _____ she wrote. "I'm having fun. I _____ you don't miss me too much!

THURSDAY — PHONICS PRACTICE

Read the story and answer the questions.

Joe

Joe lives in the country. He loves to work in the garden and to hoe the ground to plant. He loves animals and watching the buck and doe deer. He takes off his shoes and tiptoes to get close to the deer. He is a poet and writes poems about his life in the country.

1. Where does Joe live?
_____

2. What does Joe love to do in the garden?
_____

3. How does Joe get close to the deer?
_____

4. What is a synonym for doe?
Ⓐ baby Ⓑ rabbit Ⓒ deer Ⓓ saw

Circle all of the oe words in the story and then write the words in the box below.

Grade 3 Phonics and Spelling Workbook *Created by Mrs. Indira Coleby-Demeritte*

UNIT 7 Long Vowel O Page 36

ASSESSMENT

Date: _____   Score: _____

Use a red crayon to color the pictures that have the /ŏ/ (short o) sound in their name.
Use a blue crayon to color the pictures that have the /ō/ (long o) sound in their name.

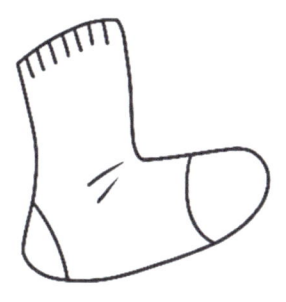

Grade 3 Phonics and Spelling Workbook   *Created by Mrs. Indira Coleby-Demeritte*

UNIT 8 Long Vowel U — Page 37

MONDAY — PHONICS PRACTICE

Write the letters u – e to complete each picture name that has the long u sound.

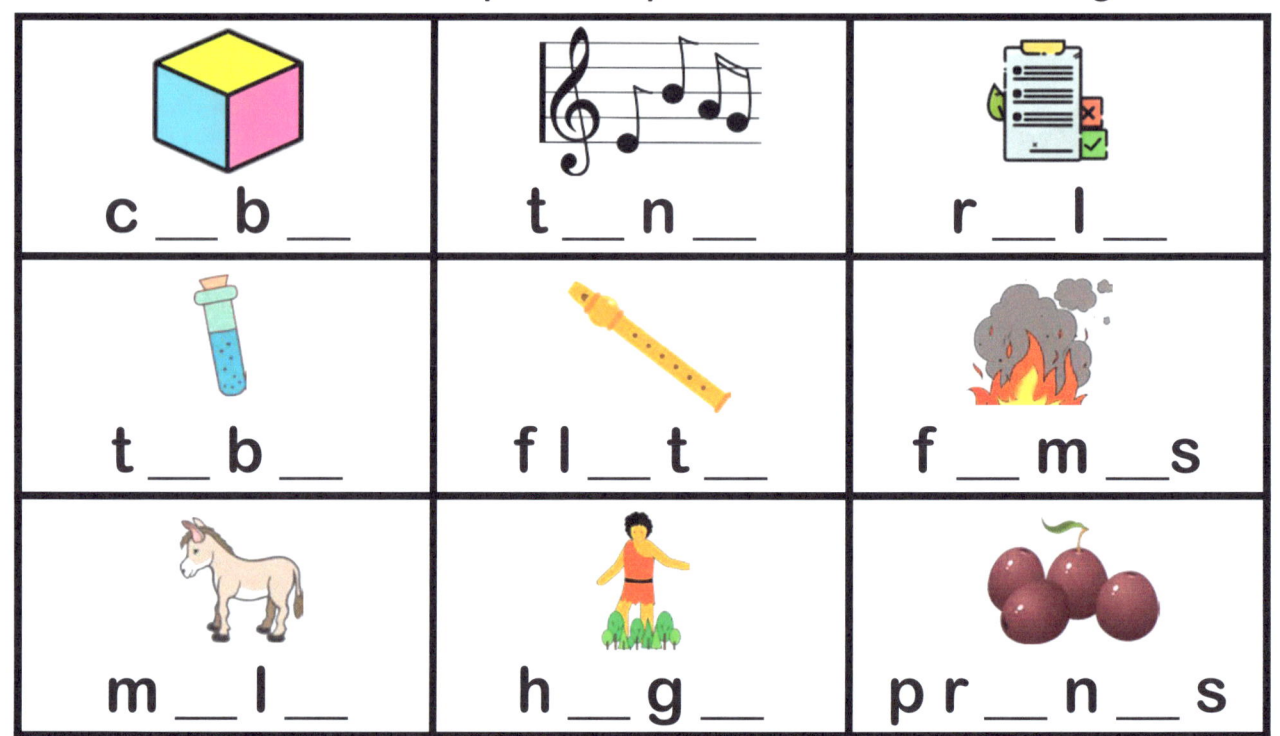

c _ b _	t _ n _	r _ l _
t _ b _	f l _ t _	f _ m _ s
m _ l _	h _ g _	p r _ n _ s

TUESDAY — PHONICS PRACTICE

Fill in the circle next to the name of each picture.

- ○ fruit / ○ foot
- ○ mice / ○ mute
- ○ juice / ○ juse
- ○ bloo / ○ blue
- ○ suit / ○ sute
- ○ glue / ○ gloo

Grade 3 Phonics and Spelling Workbook — Created by Mrs. Indira Coleby-Demeritte

UNIT 8 Long Vowel U

Page 38

WEDNESDAY — PHONICS PRACTICE

Look at the word bank. Use the words to fill in the blanks. Then read the story!

| flute | mule | Luke | tune | use |

My Pet Mule

I have a pet _____ named _____. He has many special talents.
Luke can hum a _____.
He can play the _____.
He even knows how to _____ a computer. What an amazing and amusing mule!

THURSDAY — PHONICS PRACTICE

Read the story and answer the questions.

The Cruise

We are going on a cruise. We can eat fruit and drink fruit juice by the sea. I can't forget my swim suit, as we are packing to go on our cruise. I cannot wait to sit back, sipping on my fruit juice, playing in the water with my swim suit on the cruise ship by the sea.

1. Where are we going?
_____

2. What will we get to eat and drink on the cruise?
_____

3. What can I not forget as I pack for the cruise?
_____

4. What is a synonym for cruise?
Ⓐ plane Ⓑ car Ⓒ boat trip Ⓓ hike

Circle all of the ui words in the story and then write the words in the box below.

Grade 3 Phonics and Spelling Workbook   Created by Mrs. Indira Coleby-Demeritte

UNIT 8 Long Vowel U — Page 39

ASSESSMENT

Date: _____   Score: _____

Directions: Complete each sentence below by writing the word that names the **long Uu** picture.

| duet   flute   Utah   uniforms   tuba   June   tune |

1. Next _____ the band will go on a trip.

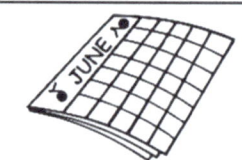

2. They will travel to _____ .

3. The band will wear their new _____ .

4. Jewel will be playing the _____ .

5. Raul will play the _____ .

6. The band will play a happy _____ .

7. Sue and Jude will sing a _____ .

Grade 3 Phonics and Spelling Workbook   *Created by Mrs. Indira Coleby-Demeritte*

UNIT 7 & 8 Long Vowel O & U

Page 40

MONDAY — SPELLING PRACTICE

Use your spelling list to write the spelling for the picture.

(cone) _____	(toe) _____	(swimsuit) _____
(cruise) _____	(crying boy) _____	(tissue) _____
(fruit) _____	(backbone) _____	(doe) _____

TUESDAY — SPELLING PRACTICE

Classify the spelling words into their vowel groups.

LONG VOWEL O	LONG VOWEL U

Spelling Words

1. load
2. joke
3. toenail
4. cone
5. bathrobe
6. doe
7. soap
8. backbone
9. goal
10. hopeful
11. fruit
12. cruise
13. argue
14. bruise
15. mule
16. ruin
17. tissue
18. swimsuit
19. huge
20. cube

Grade 3 Phonics and Spelling Workbook *Created by Mrs. Indira Coleby-Demeritte*

UNIT 7 & 8 Long Vowel O & U

WEDNESDAY — SPELLING PRACTICE

Unscramble the spelling words. The first letter is underlined.

1. polufe<u>h</u> _____
2. ul<u>m</u>e _____
3. neo<u>b</u>bcka _____
4. oelian<u>t</u> _____
5. <u>c</u>uisre _____
6. uises<u>t</u> _____
7. gu<u>a</u>re _____
8. o<u>d</u>e _____
9. ui<u>f</u>tr _____
10. hbat<u>b</u>oer _____

THURSDAY — SPELLING PRACTICE

Look at the first letter of each word. Write the words in Alphabetical Order. The alphabet chart below will help you.

A B C D **E** F G H **I** J K L M N **O** P Q R S T **U** V W X Y Z

1. argue
2. ruin
3. joke
4. bruise
5. tissue

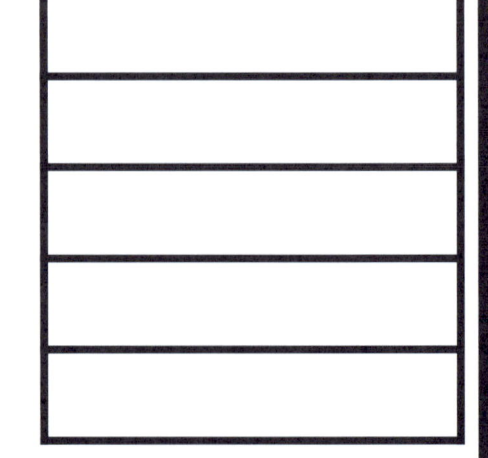

Spelling Words

1. load
2. joke
3. toenail
4. cone
5. bathrobe
6. doe
7. soap
8. backbone
9. goal
10. hopeful
11. fruit
12. cruise
13. argue
14. bruise
15. mule
16. ruin
17. tissue
18. swimsuit
19. huge
20. cube

UNIT 7 & 8 Long Vowel O & U

Practice the spelling of each word below by writing it in it's column.

load	doe	fruit	ruin	joke

soap	cruise	tissue	toenail	backbone

Grade 3 Phonics and Spelling Workbook   *Created by Mrs. Indira Coleby-Demeritte*

UNIT 7 & 8 Long Vowel O & U

Practice the spelling of each word below by writing it in it's column.

argue	swimsuit	cone	goal	bruise

huge	bathrobe	hopeful	mule	cube

UNIT 9 Syllables — Page 44

MONDAY — PHONICS PRACTICE

Syllables are the sound breaks in a word. Each syllable has a vowel sound. Say the words to yourself and then write the number of syllables were in each word.

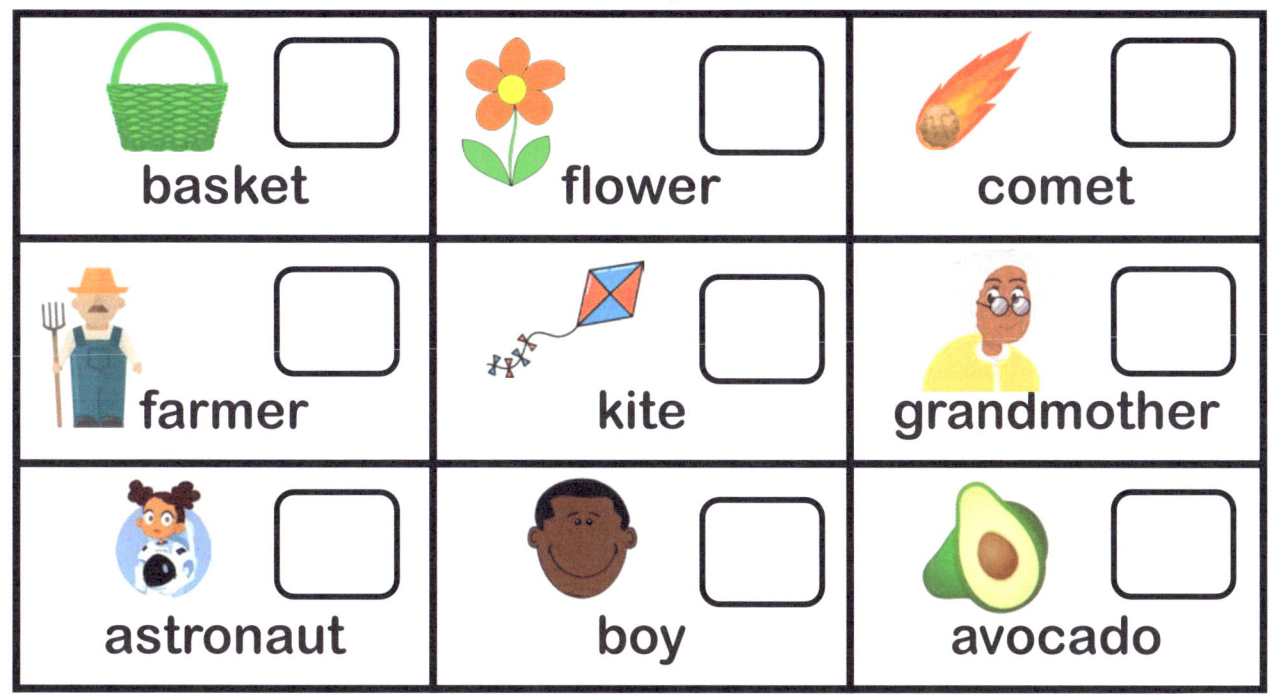

basket ☐	flower ☐	comet ☐
farmer ☐	kite ☐	grandmother ☐
astronaut ☐	boy ☐	avocado ☐

TUESDAY — PHONICS PRACTICE

One syllable rule is that we divide syllables between two middle consonants. Practice dividing the words into syllables below. The first one has been done for you.

1. basket   **bas - ket**
2. kitten _____
3. ladder _____
4. rabbit _____
5. garlic _____
6. bubble _____
7. pencil _____
8. window _____

Grade 3 Phonics and Spelling Workbook — Created by Mrs. Indira Coleby-Demeritte

UNIT 9 Syllables

Page 45

WEDNESDAY — PHONICS PRACTICE

Another syllable rule is when we have two vowels sounds in the middle of a word, we split the word so that each vowel sound is on either side of the word. Look at each picture, say the word to yourself and then divide the word into syllables. The first one has been done for you.

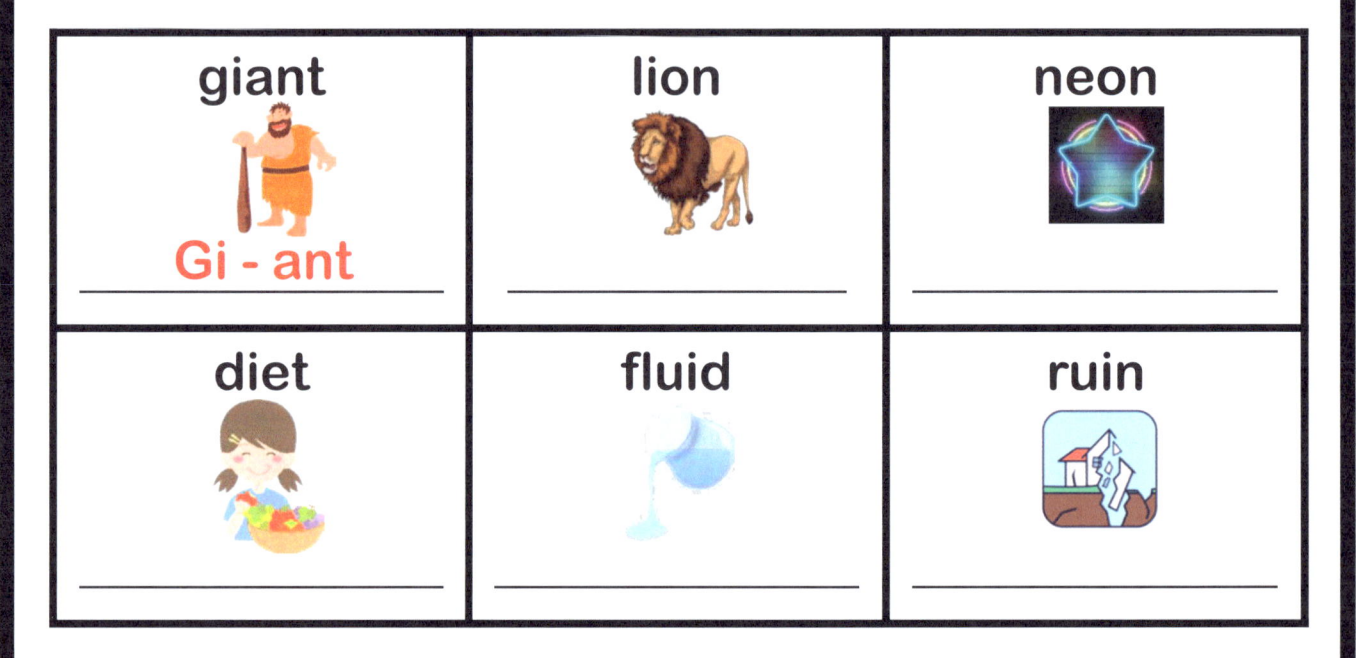

giant	lion	neon
Gi - ant		
diet	fluid	ruin

THURSDAY — PHONICS PRACTICE

Another syllable rule is that we divide after the consonant when the first vowel has a short sound. Read the words below and then divide them into syllables. The first one has been done for you.

1. camel — cam - el
2. lemon
3. comic
4. cabin
5. planet
6. wagon
7. robin
8. visit

Grade 3 Phonics and Spelling Workbook — Created by Mrs. Indira Coleby-Demeritte

UNIT 9 Syllables — Page 46

ASSESSMENT

Date: _____   Score: _____

Look at the pictures and read each word. Write the number of syllables each word has.

blueberry ☐	crocodile ☐
astronaut ☐	notebook ☐
peach ☐	helicopter ☐

A syllable rule is that we divide after the consonant when the first vowel has a short sound. Read the words below and then divide them into syllables.

1. model   _____
2. talent   _____
3. finish   _____
4. salad   _____
5. novel   _____
6. limit   _____

Grade 3 Phonics and Spelling Workbook   *Created by Mrs. Indira Coleby-Demeritte*

UNIT 9 Syllables

MONDAY — SPELLING PRACTICE

Classify the spelling words according to how many syllables each word has.

2 Syllables	3 Syllables	4 Syllables

TUESDAY — SPELLING PRACTICE

We can also divide compound words into syllables. Read the words below and divide the compound words.

1. backbone _____
2. necktie _____
3. pinecone _____

The first word in these compounds have just one syllable, but the second word has more than one syllable. Say the words carefully to yourself and divide the words into syllables.

4. strawberry _____
5. ecosystem _____

Spelling Words

1. January
2. backbone
3. amphibians
4. Abaco
5. necktie
6. raise
7. teacher
8. kneel
9. pinecone
10. cone
11. rocky
12. strawberry
13. battery
14. Bimini
15. caterpillar
16. cereal
17. celery
18. ice
19. ecosystem
20. butterfly

Grade 3 Phonics and Spelling Workbook   Created by Mrs. Indira Coleby-Demeritte

UNIT 9 Syllables   Page 48

WEDNESDAY — SPELLING PRACTICE

Use the word box to write a rhyming word for the words below.

| cone | rocky | kneel |
| ice | raise | teacher |

1. preacher _____
2. Steel _____
3. nice _____
4. maze _____
5. stocky _____
6. zone _____

THURSDAY — SPELLING PRACTICE

Look at the first letter of each word. Write the words in Alphabetical Order. The alphabet chart below will help you.

A B C D E F G H I J K L M N O P Q R S T U V W X Y Z

1. caterpillar
2. ecosystem
3. amphibians
4. January
5. Bimini

Spelling Words

1. January
2. backbone
3. amphibians
4. Abaco
5. necktie
6. raise
7. teacher
8. kneel
9. pinecone
10. cone
11. rocky
12. strawberry
13. battery
14. Bimini
15. caterpillar
16. cereal
17. celery
18. ice
19. ecosystem
20. butterfly

Grade 3 Phonics and Spelling Workbook   Created by Mrs. Indira Coleby-Demeritte

UNIT 9 Syllables — Page 49

Practice the spelling of each word below by writing it in it's column.

January	Abaco	kneel	strawberry	cereal

butterfly	necktie	pinecone	battery	celery

Grade 3 Phonics and Spelling Workbook *Created by Mrs. Indira Coleby-Demeritte*

UNIT 9 Syllables

Practice the spelling of each word below by writing it in it's column.

backbone	raise	cone	Bimini	ice

amphibians	teacher	rocky	caterpillar	ecosystem

UNIT 10 Syllables Page 51

MONDAY — PHONICS PRACTICE

A syllable rule is that we divide before the consonant if the first vowel has a long sound. Look at each word and picture and draw a slash to separate the syllables. The first one has been done for you.

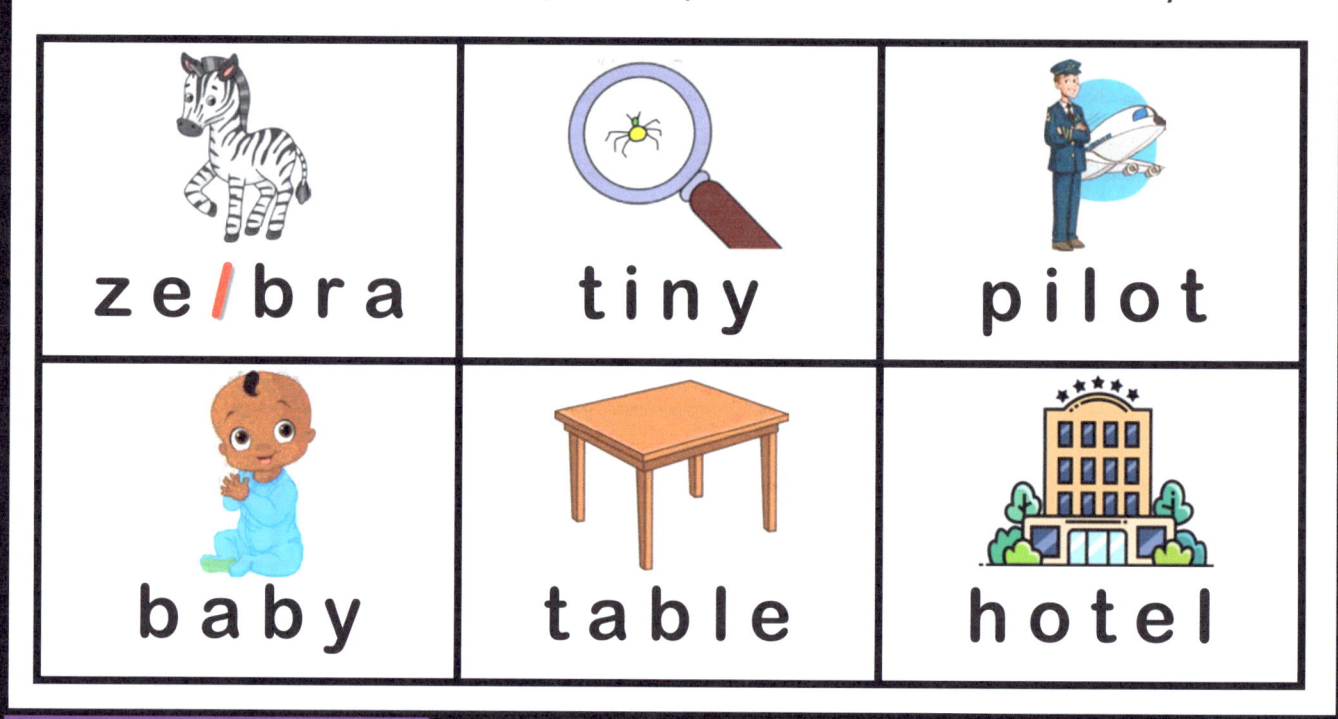

ze/bra	tiny	pilot
baby	table	hotel

TUESDAY — PHONICS PRACTICE

Another syllable rule is that we divide a syllable after a prefix and before a suffix. Read the words below and then divide them into syllables. The first one has been done for you.

1. unable   un- able
2. unkind   _____
3. replay   _____
4. joyful   _____
5. review   _____
6. tallest   _____
7. preheat   _____
8. friendly   _____

Grade 3 Phonics and Spelling Workbook   *Created by Mrs. Indira Coleby-Demeritte*

UNIT 10 Syllables

WEDNESDAY — PHONICS PRACTICE

A syllable rule is that we keep digraphs together when we separate syllables. Look at the pictures and words below and use a slash to separate each syllable. The first one has been done for you.

 broth/er	 nephew	 cashew
 mother	 gather	 fashion

THURSDAY — PHONICS PRACTICE

Read the poem. Then, complete each sentence by writing the correct word from the poem on the line.

Jack Be Nimble

Jack be nimble,
Jack be quick.
Jack jump over
The candlestick

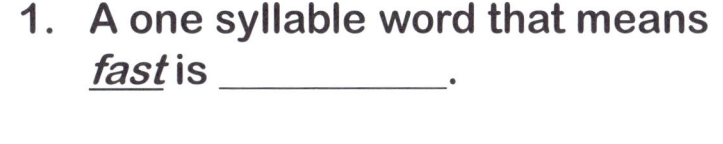

1. A one syllable word that means *fast* is _____.

2. The two syllable word in the *title* of the poem is _____.

3. The *three syllable* word in the poem is _____.

4. A two syllable word that means *above or across* is _____.

Grade 3 Phonics and Spelling Workbook   *Created by Mrs. Indira Coleby-Demeritte*

UNIT 10 Syllables

ASSESSMENT

Date: _____   Score: _____

Say the word, clap out the syllables. Write the number of syllables on the line.

1. Atlantic _____
2. order _____
3. greatest _____
4. ascending _____
5. addition _____

6. Bahamas _____
7. apple _____
8. saturday _____
9. calculator _____
10. marlin _____

Circle the correct word that shows the correct division of syllables.

Purple 
a. pu-r-ple
b. pur-ple

Yellow 
a. yel-low
b. yell-ow

Flamingo 
a. fla-min-go
b. f-la-ming-o

Cylinder 
a. cylin-der
b. cy-lin-der

Divide the words below into syllables.

15. baby _____   16. pencil _____

Grade 3 Phonics and Spelling Workbook   *Created by Mrs. Indira Coleby-Demeritte*

UNIT 10 Syllables

Page 54

MONDAY — SPELLING PRACTICE

Look at each picture and then write the spelling word that matches it.

(flag) _____	(smiley) _____	(pencil) _____
(marlin) _____	(apple) _____	(beetle) _____
(baby) _____	(calculator) _____	(addition) _____

TUESDAY — SPELLING PRACTICE

Classify the spelling words according to how many syllables each word has.

2 Syllables	3 Syllables

Spelling Words

1. Atlantic
2. order
3. greatest
4. ascending
5. addition
6. Bahamas
7. baby
8. pencil
9. apple
10. yellow
11. Saturday
12. October
13. purple
14. cylinder
15. happy
16. beetle
17. flamingo
18. marlin
19. library
20. calculator

Grade 3 Phonics and Spelling Workbook — Created by Mrs. Indira Coleby-Demeritte

UNIT 10 Syllables

WEDNESDAY — SPELLING PRACTICE

Look at the first letter of each word. Write the words in Alphabetical Order. The alphabet chart below will help you.

A B C D E F G H I J K L M N O P Q R S T U V W X Y Z

1. Bahamas
2. ascending
3. Saturday
4. calculator
5. flamingo
6. October

THURSDAY — SPELLING PRACTICE

Synonyms are words that have almost the same meaning. Use the word box to write the synonyms for the words below.

baby	addition	greatest
happy	order	beetle

1. plus _____
2. sequence _____
3. ecstatic _____
4. bug _____
5. infant _____
6. biggest _____

Spelling Words

1. Atlantic
2. order
3. greatest
4. ascending
5. addition
6. Bahamas
7. baby
8. pencil
9. apple
10. yellow
11. Saturday
12. October
13. purple
14. cylinder
15. happy
16. beetle
17. flamingo
18. marlin
19. library
20. calculator

UNIT 10 Syllables — Page 56

Practice the spelling of each word below by writing it in it's column.

Atlantic	addition	apple	purple	flamingo

order	Bahamas	yellow	cylinder	marlin

Grade 3 Phonics and Spelling Workbook — *Created by Mrs. Indira Coleby-Demeritte*

UNIT 10 Syllables

Practice the spelling of each word below by writing it in it's column.

calculator	greatest	baby	Saturday	happy

library	ascending	pencil	October	beetle

UNIT 11 Y As Long Vowel E & I — Page 58

MONDAY — PHONICS PRACTICE

When Y is at the end of a one-syllable word, it often stands for the long I sound. Write y to complete each picture name that ends with the long I sound.

| fr __ | sk __ | fl __ |
| cr __ | dr __ | sp __ |

TUESDAY — PHONICS PRACTICE

When the letter Y is at the end of a two-syllable word, it usually stands for the long e sound. Write y to complete each picture name that ends with the long e sound.

| famil __ | cit __ | bunn __ |
| pupp __ | funn __ | angr __ |

Grade 3 Phonics and Spelling Workbook *Created by Mrs. Indira Coleby-Demeritte*

UNIT 11 Y As Long Vowel E & I — Page 59

WEDNESDAY — PHONICS PRACTICE

Look at each picture, then circle whether the Y is making the long e or long I sound.

(candy)	(crying baby)	(sun)
 Long E Long I	 Long E Long I	 Long E Long I
(sky with clouds)	(fly)	(spy)
 Long E Long I	 Long E Long I	 Long E Long I

THURSDAY — PHONICS PRACTICE

Read the story and answer the questions.

The Python

"Don't cry!" said the python. "I am very shy." The python crawled by the rabbit on the dry ground, as the sun went up in the sky. The rabbit did not trust the sly python, so it hopped away.

1. Who said, "Don't cry!"?
   _____

2. Where did the python crawl by the rabbit?
   _____

3. Why did the rabbit hop away?
   _____

4. What is a synonym for sly?
   Ⓐ crawl Ⓑ long Ⓒ clever Ⓓ nice

Circle all of the y as long I words in the story and then write the words in the box below.

Grade 3 Phonics and Spelling Workbook — Created by Mrs. Indira Coleby-Demeritte

| UNIT 11 Y As Long Vowel E & I | Page 60 |

ASSESSMENT

Date: _____   Score: _____

Read the poem below and use the word box to complete it. Then fill in the sentences below using words from the poem.

| try | why | sky | by | fly |

CLOUDS

I like to look up in the _____,
To see animals flying _____.
Dogs and cats and cows and pigs,
All _____ by and look so big!

My eyes see animals near and far.
I _____ to think of what they are.
_____, I ask, do animals try,
To look like clouds up in the sky?

1. The animals fly by in the _____.

2. I _____ to watch them.

3. I use _____ eyes to see the animals.

4. The animals _____ to look like clouds!

UNIT 11 Y As Long Vowel E & I

Page 61

MONDAY — SPELLING PRACTICE

Look at each picture and then write the spelling word that matches it.

TUESDAY — SPELLING PRACTICE

Classify the spelling words to show which sound Y makes in each word. Write the words in the boxes below.

Y as Long Vowel E	Y as Long Vowel I

Spelling Words

1. money
2. dry
3. cheery
4. dragonfly
5. berry
6. every
7. grouchy
8. February
9. July
10. valley
11. sorry
12. lazy
13. body
14. cloudy
15. comply
16. penny
17. shy
18. reply
19. spry
20. supply

Grade 3 Phonics and Spelling Workbook   *Created by Mrs. Indira Coleby-Demeritte*

UNIT 11 Y As Long Vowel E & I — Page 62

WEDNESDAY — SPELLING PRACTICE

Use the word box to write a synonym for the words listed below.

money	penny	cheery
reply	spry	grouchy

1. one cent _____
2. answering _____
3. cash _____
4. irritated _____
5. happy _____
6. light rain _____

THURSDAY — SPELLING PRACTICE

Divide each word below into syllables.

1. sorry _____
2. penny _____
3. berry _____
4. money _____
5. comply _____
6. reply _____
7. July _____
8. dragonfly _____

Spelling Words

1. money
2. dry
3. cheery
4. dragonfly
5. berry
6. every
7. grouchy
8. February
9. July
10. valley
11. sorry
12. lazy
13. body
14. cloudy
15. comply
16. penny
17. shy
18. reply
19. spry
20. supply

Grade 3 Phonics and Spelling Workbook   *Created by Mrs. Indira Coleby-Demeritte*

UNIT 11 Y As Long Vowel E & I — Page 63

Practice the spelling of each word below by writing it in it's column.

money	dry	cheery	dragonfly	berry

every	grouchy	February	July	valley

Grade 3 Phonics and Spelling Workbook *Created by Mrs. Indira Coleby-Demeritte*

UNIT 11 Y As Long Vowel E & I — Page 64

Practice the spelling of each word below by writing it in it's column.

sorry	lazy	body	cloudy	comply

penny	shy	reply	spry	supply

Grade 3 Phonics and Spelling Workbook — *Created by Mrs. Indira Coleby-Demeritte*

UNIT 12 Hard and Soft C & G   Page 65

MONDAY — PHONICS PRACTICE

When the letter c is followed by the vowels e, i or y is has a soft sound. Soft C sounds like the letter s, hard c sounds like the letter k. Look at each picture and word below, then write if the letter c is making a hard or soft sound in the word.

celery	cap	pencil
_____	_____	_____
cow	cub	ice
_____	_____	_____

TUESDAY — PHONICS PRACTICE

When the letter g is followed by the vowels e, i or y is has a soft sound. Soft g sounds like the letter j. Look at each picture, then circle if the word is making a hard or soft sound.

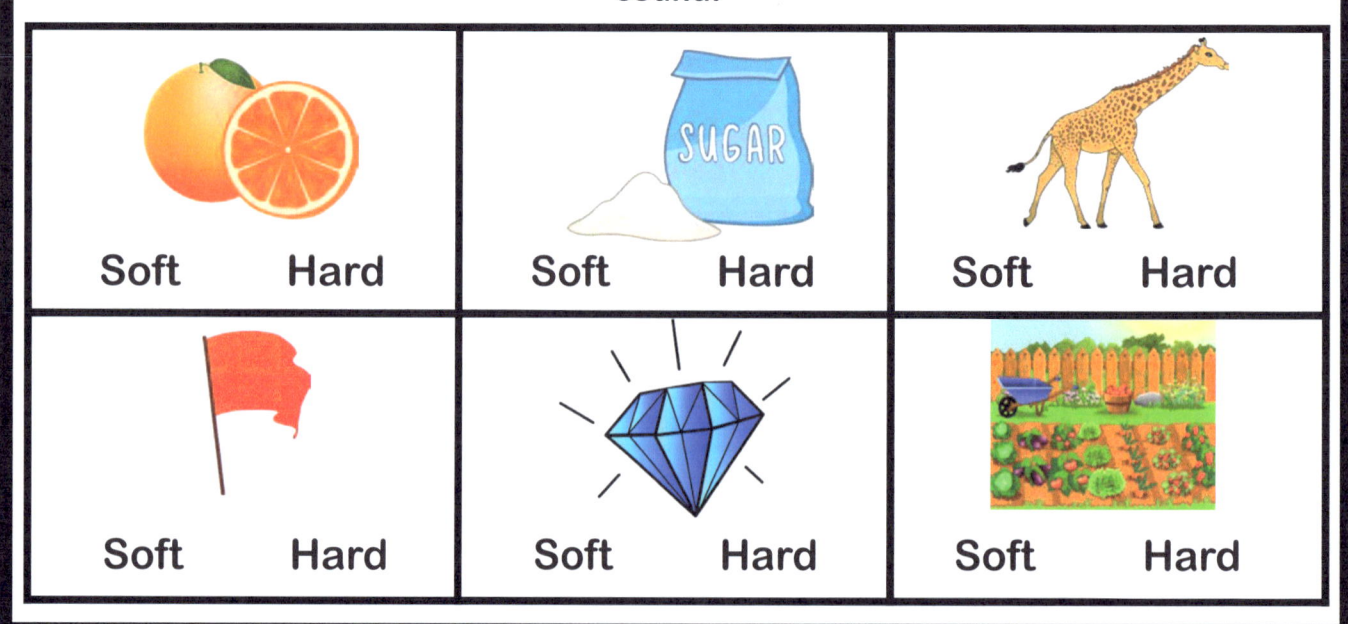

Soft Hard	Soft Hard	Soft Hard
(orange)	(sugar)	(giraffe)
Soft Hard	Soft Hard	Soft Hard
(flag)	(diamond)	(garden)

Grade 3 Phonics and Spelling Workbook   Created by Mrs. Indira Coleby-Demeritte

UNIT 12 Hard and Soft C & G

Page 66

WEDNESDAY — PHONICS PRACTICE

Color the picture that has either a hard c sound red, color the picture that has a soft c sound blue.

cake · cider · cat  · cart

coat  · cylinder · cone  · cereal

THURSDAY — PHONICS PRACTICE

Say the words to yourself and then draw a line to connect the words that have the same g sound in each set.

page	game	figure	large
flag	engine	gold	giraffe
orange	gym	gutter	ago
sugar	organ	pigeon	arrange

Grade 3 Phonics and Spelling Workbook — Created by Mrs. Indira Coleby-Demeritte

UNIT 12 Hard and Soft C & G

ASSESSMENT

Date: _____   Score: _____

Fill in the circle beside the word that belongs in each sentence.

1. Alice _____ a package for her birthday.
   ○ got   ○ gym

2. She was ____ that it was from Carl.
   ○ curtain   ○ certain

3. The package was ____ !
   ○ huge   ○ hug

4. Alice tried to _____ what was in it.
   ○ gem   ○ guess

5. She _____ opened the enormous box.
   ○ cement   ○ carefully

6. A ____ orange kite was inside.
   ○ giant   ○ garden

7. "I ____ believe it," Alice exclaimed.
   ○ cent   ○ can't

8. "I'll ____ Carl right away to thank him.
   ○ call   ○ cell

Grade 3 Phonics and Spelling Workbook   Created by Mrs. Indira Coleby-Demeritte

UNIT 12 Hard and Soft C & G   Page 68

MONDAY — SPELLING PRACTICE

Look at each picture and then write the spelling word that matches it.

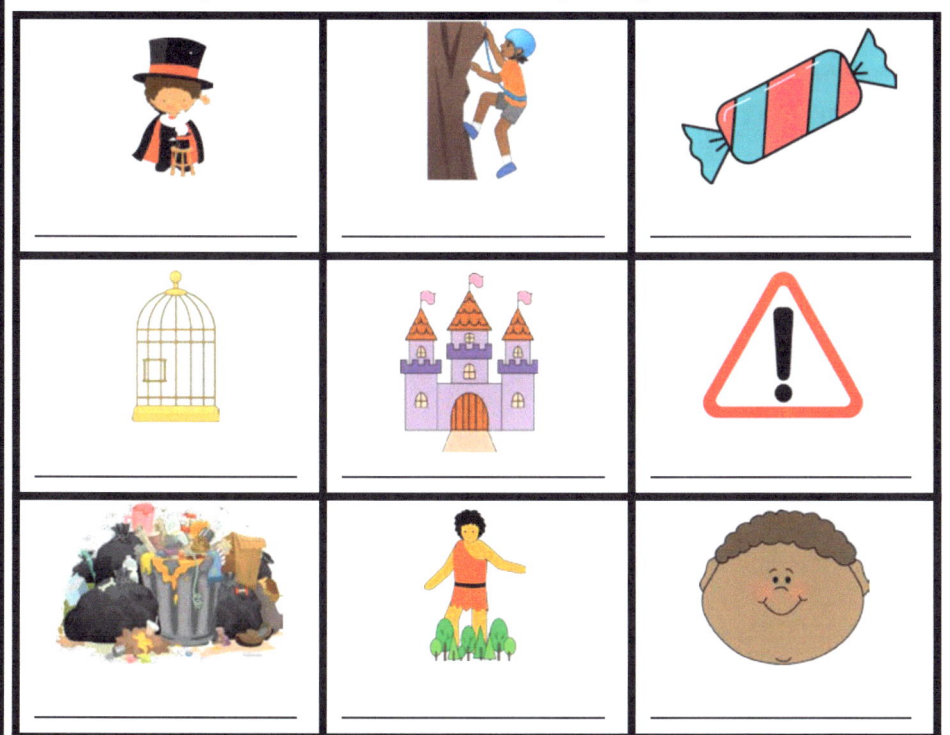

_____	_____	_____
_____	_____	_____
_____	_____	_____

TUESDAY — SPELLING PRACTICE

Classify the spelling words to show soft c and hard c.

SOFT C	HARD C

Spelling Words

1. giant
2. case
3. face
4. cage
5. country
6. once
7. climb
8. energy
9. magician
10. garbage
11. giraffe
12. fancy
13. candy
14. decide
15. castle
16. genius
17. center
18. intelligent
19. welcome
20. dangerous

Grade 3 Phonics and Spelling Workbook   *Created by Mrs. Indira Coleby-Demeritte*

UNIT 12 Hard and Soft C & G — Page 69

WEDNESDAY — SPELLING PRACTICE

Use the word box to write a synonym for the words listed below.

garbage	intelligent	center
dangerous	candy	decide

1. not safe _____
2. sweets _____
3. smart _____
4. choice _____
5. trash _____
6. middle _____

THURSDAY — SPELLING PRACTICE

Unscramble the spelling word. The first letter is underlined.

1. ba<u>g</u>earg _____
1. lcome<u>w</u>e _____
2. fe<u>g</u>raif _____
3. nt<u>c</u>oruy _____
4. <u>m</u>gicnaai _____
5. <u>g</u>eny<u>r</u>e _____
6. i<u>d</u>ecde _____
7. rgean<u>d</u>osu _____
8. <u>c</u>laste _____

Spelling Words

1. giant
2. case
3. face
4. cage
5. country
6. once
7. climb
8. energy
9. magician
10. garbage
11. giraffe
12. fancy
13. candy
14. decide
15. castle
16. genius
17. center
18. intelligent
19. welcome
20. dangerous

UNIT 12 Hard and Soft C & G — Page 70

Practice the spelling of each word below by writing it in it's column.

giant	country	magician	candy	center

case	once	garbage	decide	intelligent

Grade 3 Phonics and Spelling Workbook *Created by Mrs. Indira Coleby-Demeritte*

UNIT 12 Hard and Soft C & G — Page 71

Practice the spelling of each word below by writing it in it's column.

face	climb	giraffe	castle	welcome

cage	energy	fancy	genius	dangerous

Grade 3 Phonics and Spelling Workbook *Created by Mrs. Indira Coleby-Demeritte*

UNIT 13 R Blends

Page 72

MONDAY — PHONICS PRACTICE

Write the name of each picture. Circle the r blend that stands for the beginning sound

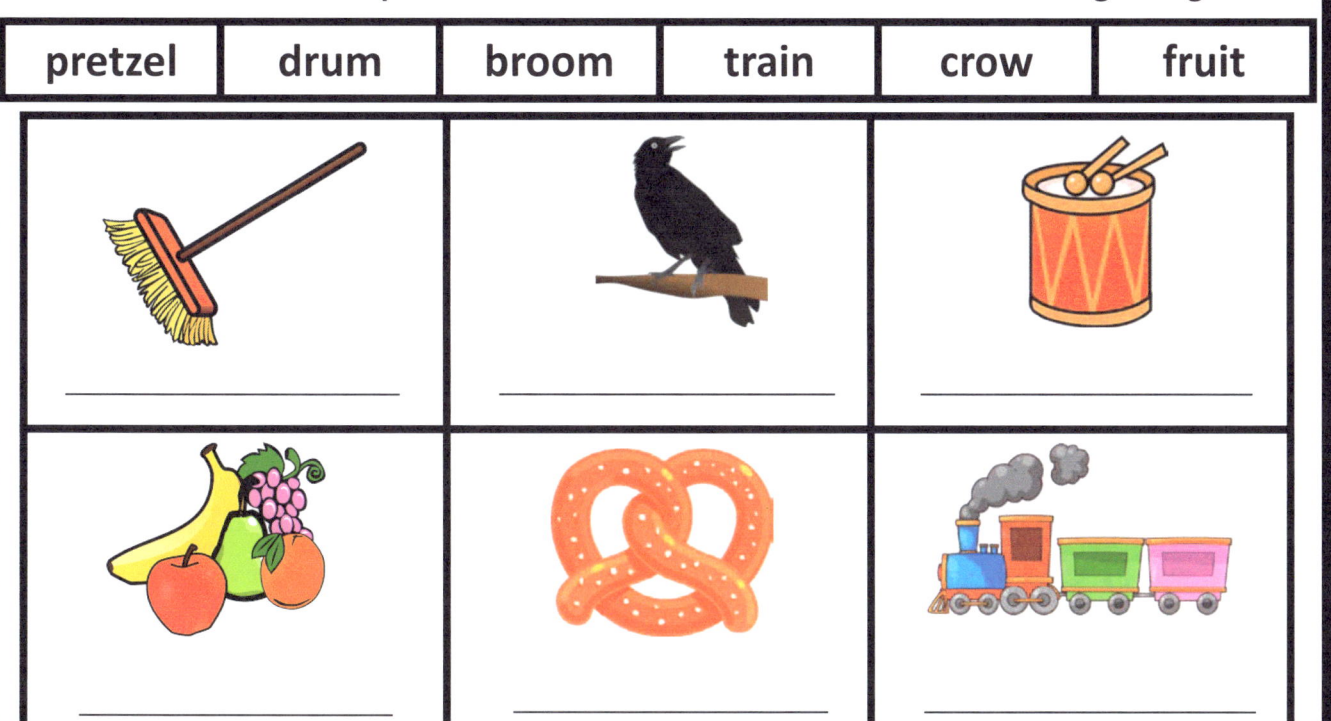

| pretzel | drum | broom | train | crow | fruit |

TUESDAY — PHONICS PRACTICE

Look at each picture and say it quietly to yourself. Then write the r-blend that you hear on the lines below.

Rr Blends

Listen for the Rr blends as in trap and grass

1.
2.
3.
4.
5.
6.
7.

Grade 3 Phonics and Spelling Workbook Created by Mrs. Indira Coleby-Demeritte

UNIT 13 R Blends — Page 73

WEDNESDAY — PHONICS PRACTICE

Look at the word bank. Use the words to fill in the blanks. Then read the story!

| brag | brave | bring | crow | cry | creek |

Silly Crow

A silly _____ lived near a _____. He liked to _____ about how great he was. "I'm so smart and _____!" he said. Soon the other birds left him alone. The crow felt sad and started to _____. "I'll stop bragging," he said. "That will _____ my friends back." And it did!

THURSDAY — PHONICS PRACTICE

Read the story and answer the questions.

Bronco, the Bear

My little brother, Brad, has a brown bear named Bronco. Brad brings Bronco with him everywhere he goes. He eats breakfast with him, goes fishing down at the brook, and takes him across the bridge on his bike. Brad loves his brown bear, Bronco.

1. What is Bronco?
   _____

2. Where does Brad take his bear to go fishing?
   _____

3. Where does Brad ride his bike?
   _____

4. What is a synonym for brook?
   Ⓐ bear Ⓑ creek Ⓒ fish Ⓓ walk

Circle all of the r-blend words in the story and then write the words in the box below.

Grade 3 Phonics and Spelling Workbook — Created by Mrs. Indira Coleby-Demeritte

UNIT 13 R Blends — Page 74

ASSESSMENT

Date: _____   Score: _____

R - Family Blends

Say the name of each picture. Circle the sound that it begins with. Then write the missing letters to complete each word.

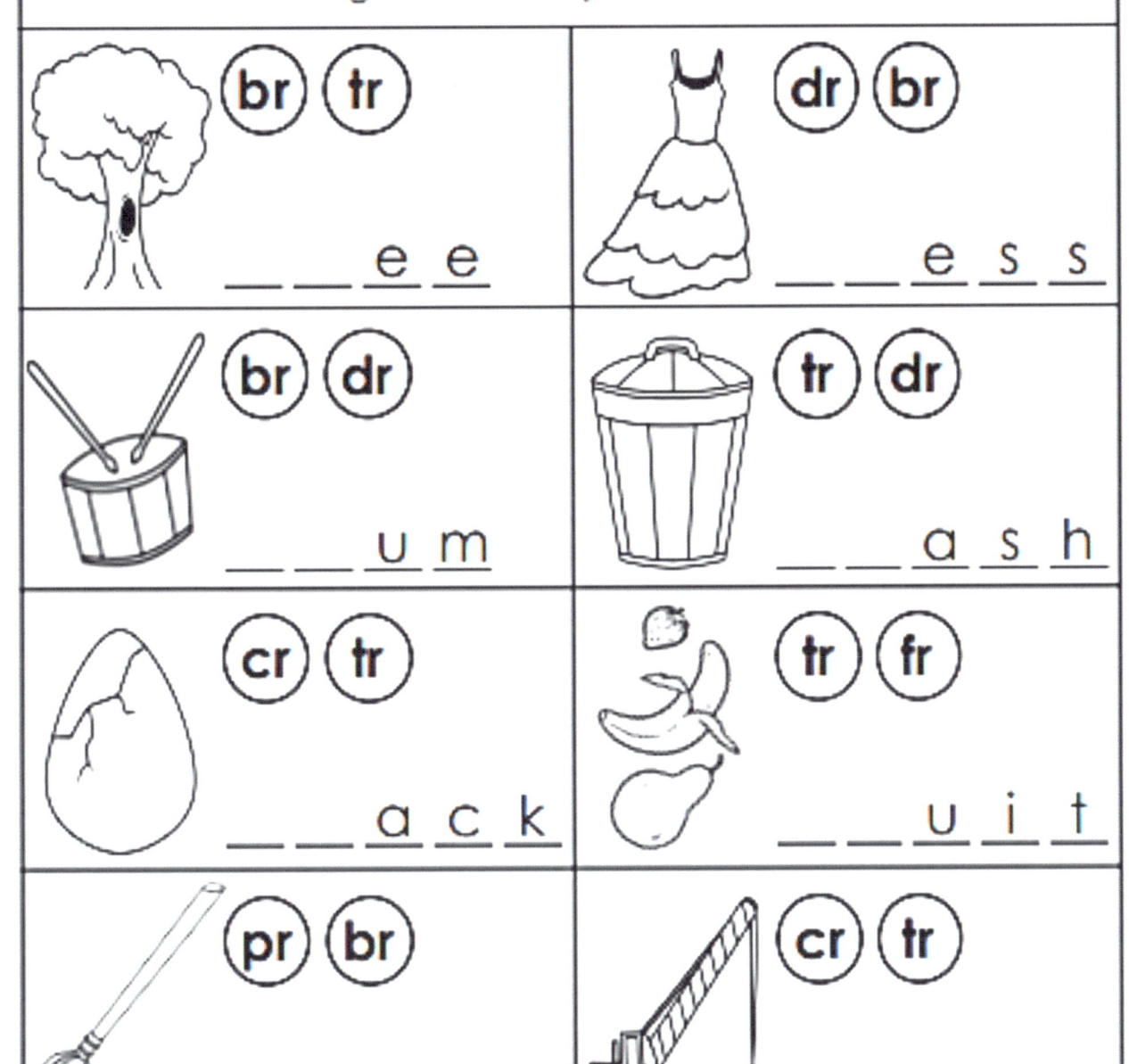

(br) (tr) __ __ e e	(dr) (br) __ __ e s s
(br) (dr) __ __ u m	(tr) (dr) __ __ a s h
(cr) (tr) __ __ a c k	(tr) (fr) __ __ u i t
(pr) (br) __ __ u s h	(cr) (tr) __ __ a n e

Grade 3 Phonics and Spelling Workbook   Created by Mrs. Indira Coleby-Demeritte

UNIT 13 R Blends   Page 75

MONDAY — SPELLING PRACTICE

Look at each picture and then write the spelling word that matches it.

TUESDAY — SPELLING PRACTICE

Look at the first letter of each word. Write the words in Alphabetical Order. The alphabet chart below will help you.

A B C D E F G H I J K L M N O P Q R S T U V W X Y Z

1. frowning
2. bravery
3. grilled
4. fragile
5. drowsy

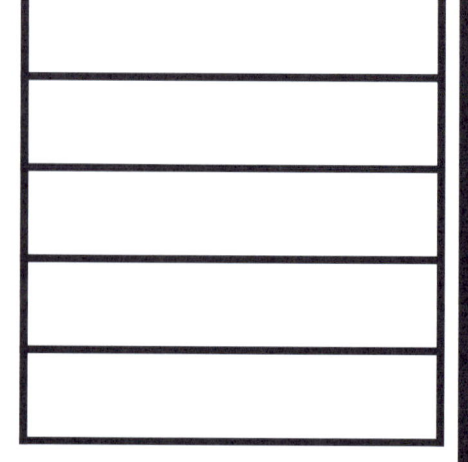

Spelling Words

1. creek
2. drowsy
3. drum
4. train
5. broom
6. fragile
7. brother
8. dream
9. grapes
10. bride
11. prize
12. frowning
13. friends
14. bravery
15. free
16. Friday
17. drove
18. fresh
19. cream
20. grilled

Grade 3 Phonics and Spelling Workbook   Created by Mrs. Indira Coleby-Demeritte

UNIT 13 R Blends — Page 76

WEDNESDAY — SPELLING PRACTICE

Use the word box to write a synonym for the words listed below.

drowsy	frowning	prize
train	free	fragile

1. gift _____
2. weak _____
3. liberate _____
4. sleepy _____
5. sad _____
6. teach _____

THURSDAY — SPELLING PRACTICE

Unscramble the spelling word. The first letter is underlined.

1. idn<u>f</u>res _____
1. r<u>b</u>rayev _____
2. ema<u>d</u>r _____
3. <u>g</u>lerafi _____
4. eker<u>c</u> _____
5. yadi<u>Fr</u> _____
6. il<u>g</u>lred _____
7. <u>b</u>heortr _____
8. gnwi<u>f</u>orn _____

Spelling Words

1. creek
2. drowsy
3. drum
4. train
5. broom
6. fragile
7. brother
8. dream
9. grapes
10. bride
11. prize
12. frowning
13. friends
14. bravery
15. free
16. Friday
17. drove
18. fresh
19. cream
20. grilled

Grade 3 Phonics and Spelling Workbook — Created by Mrs. Indira Coleby-Demeritte

UNIT 13 R Blends — Page 77

Practice the spelling of each word below by writing it in it's column.

creek	fragile	prize	Friday	drowsy

brother	frowning	drove	drum	dream

Grade 3 Phonics and Spelling Workbook — Created by Mrs. Indira Coleby-Demeritte

UNIT 13 R Blends

Practice the spelling of each word below by writing it in it's column.

friends	fresh	train	grapes	bravery

cream	broom	bride	free	grilled

Grade 3 Phonics and Spelling Workbook — *Created by Mrs. Indira Coleby-Demeritte*

UNIT 14 L Blends

Page 79

MONDAY — PHONICS PRACTICE

Write the name of each picture. Circle the L blend that stands for the beginning sound

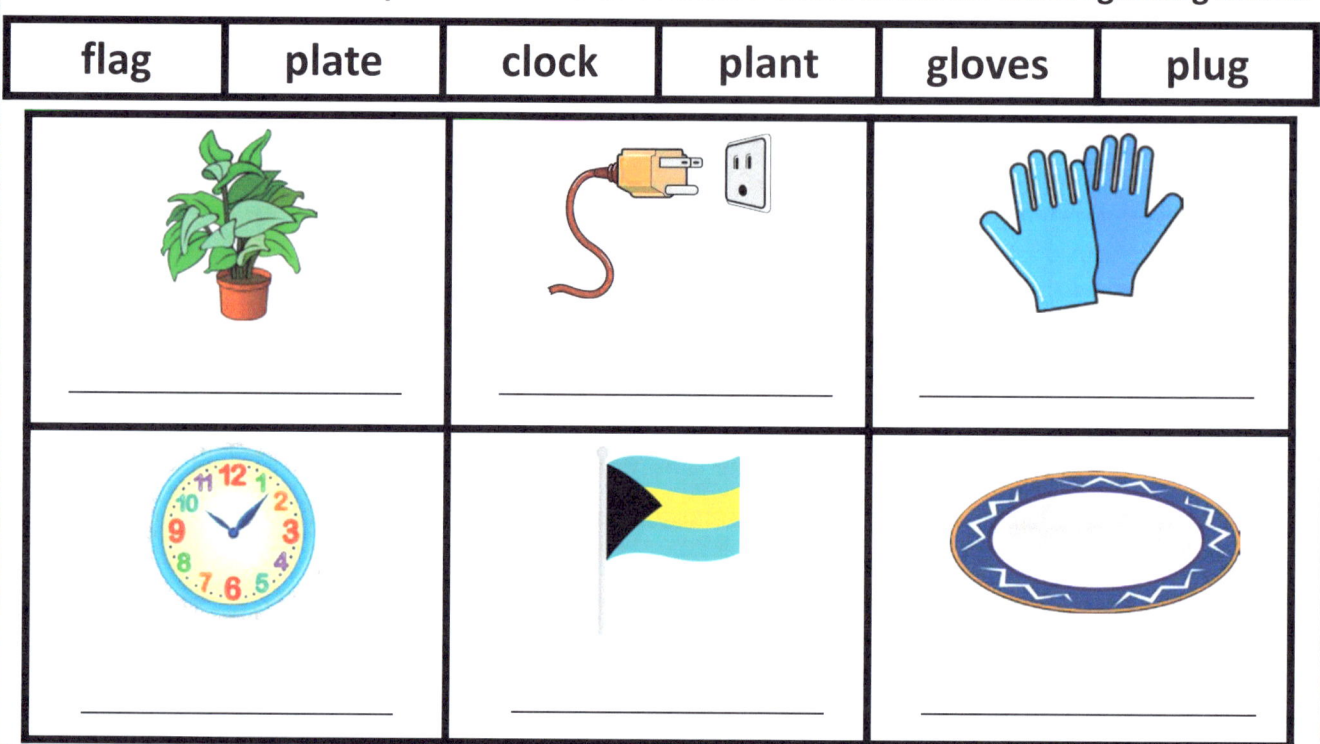

| flag | plate | clock | plant | gloves | plug |

TUESDAY — PHONICS PRACTICE

Look at each picture and say it quietly to yourself. Then write the l-blend that you hear on the lines below.

Ll Blends

Listen for the Ll blends as in flag and slide.

1.
2.
3.
4.
5.
6.
7.

Grade 3 Phonics and Spelling Workbook — Created by Mrs. Indira Coleby-Demeritte

UNIT 14 L Blends

WEDNESDAY — PHONICS PRACTICE

Look at the word bank. Use the words to fill in the blanks. Then read the story!

| blanket | blue | float | fly | places | plane |

Fly Away

I was on a _____ for the first time. We were going to Florida to visit Grandma. I got a pillow and a _____. I looked out the window at the _____ sky. I saw fluffy clouds _____ by. It's fun to _____ to new _____!

THURSDAY — PHONICS PRACTICE

When a consonant is followed by the letter l at the beginning of a word, blend the sounds of the letters. Circle and write the letters that complete each word and write it on the line.

1. The boy watched his __ __ock of sheep.   pl fl cl
2. One of the sheep ran to the __ __iff.   cl fl bl
3. The little __ __ack sheep did not come back.   pl bl cl
4. The boy heard a __ __ock ring out the time.   cl pl bl
5. The boy began to __ __ink his eyes.   pl gl bl
6. Then he saw the sheep on a __ __at rock.   fl bl cl
7. He climbed up to the sheep and said   pl gl bl
   "__ __ease come back."

Grade 3 Phonics and Spelling Workbook   Created by Mrs. Indira Coleby-Demeritte

UNIT 14 L Blends — Page 81

ASSESSMENT

Date: _____   Score: _____

L-Family Blends

Say the name of each picture. Circle the sound that it begins with.

Picture	Choices	Picture	Choices	Picture	Choices
(plate)	bl / cl / pl	(flag)	bl / fl / pl	(shirt/clothes)	cl / pl / sl
(flower)	fl / gl / pl	(block)	bl / pl / sl	(plug)	bl / cl / pl
(slide)	cl / fl / sl	(glue)	cl / gl / sl	(clock)	cl / fl / sl

Grade 3 Phonics and Spelling Workbook   Created by Mrs. Indira Coleby-Demeritte

UNIT 14 L Blends

Page 82

MONDAY — SPELLING PRACTICE

Look at each picture and then write the spelling word that matches it.

_____	_____	_____
_____	_____	_____
_____	_____	_____

TUESDAY — SPELLING PRACTICE

Use the word box to write the rhyming word for the words listed below.

flower	please	flood
cloud	blender	flight

1. tender _____
2. mud _____
3. power _____
4. tease _____
5. tight _____
6. proud _____

Spelling Words

1. gloomy
2. flight
3. gladiator
4. plants
5. glasses
6. flood
7. slumber
8. blender
9. blindfold
10. blueberry
11. clothes
12. clever
13. flower
14. glitter
15. plenty
16. sleeve
17. slower
18. cloud
19. please
20. plural

Grade 3 Phonics and Spelling Workbook *Created by Mrs. Indira Coleby-Demeritte*

UNIT 14 L Blends   Page 83

WEDNESDAY — SPELLING PRACTICE

Use the word box to write a synonym for the words listed below.

gladiator	gloomy	blender
slumber	plural	flight

1. trip _____
2. sleep _____
3. warrior _____
4. many _____
5. unhappy _____
6. mixer _____

THURSDAY — SPELLING PRACTICE

Divide each word below into syllables.

1. slumber _____
2. clever _____
3. plenty _____
4. glitter _____
5. blueberry _____
6. blindfold _____
7. blender _____
8. gladiator _____

Spelling Words

1. gloomy
2. flight
3. gladiator
4. plants
5. glasses
6. flood
7. slumber
8. blender
9. blindfold
10. blueberry
11. clothes
12. clever
13. flower
14. glitter
15. plenty
16. sleeve
17. slower
18. cloud
19. please
20. plural

Grade 3 Phonics and Spelling Workbook   Created by Mrs. Indira Coleby-Demeritte

UNIT 14 L Blends — Page 84

Practice the spelling of each word below by writing it in it's column.

gloomy	flood	clothes	sleeve	flight

slumber	clever	slower	gladiator	blender

Grade 3 Phonics and Spelling Workbook — Created by Mrs. Indira Coleby-Demeritte

UNIT 14 L Blends — Page 85

Practice the spelling of each word below by writing it in it's column.

flower	cloud	plants	blindfold	glitter

please	glasses	blueberry	plenty	plural

Grade 3 Phonics and Spelling Workbook — Created by Mrs. Indira Coleby-Demeritte

UNIT 15 S Blends

Page 86

MONDAY — PHONICS PRACTICE

Color the circle that shows the s-blend for each picture.

(skate) sk / sp	(slippers) sp / sl	(spaceship) st / sp
(stop) sl / st	(swan) sw / sm	(stones) sk / st

TUESDAY — PHONICS PRACTICE

Circle the word that has the correct blend to match the picture. Then write the s-blend on the lines below.

(smile face) smile / skile	(stamp) slamp / stamp	(sled) sled / sped
(snake) snake / stake	(sky) sky / smy	(spoon) sroon / spoon

Grade 3 Phonics and Spelling Workbook — Created by Mrs. Indira Coleby-Demeritte

UNIT 15 S Blends

Page 87

WEDNESDAY — PHONICS PRACTICE

Look at each picture and word, then use them to complete the sentences below.

spoon   spin   spots   spill

1. My toy top can _____.
2. Don't _____ the water.
3. I eat soup with a _____.
4. My dog has _____.

THURSDAY — PHONICS PRACTICE

Read the story and answer the questions.

Snoopy

Snoopy wanted to go outside and play in the snow. He wanted to build a snowman. Snoopy snatched a hat, gloves, and a scarf. He played in the snow. Snoopy sneezes and starts to sniffle. He came inside to get a snack and snuggle by the fireplace.

1. What does Snoopy want to build?
_____

2. What did Snoopy start to do after he sneezed?
_____

3. What did Snoopy snuggle by when he came inside?
_____

4. What is a synonym for snatch?
Ⓐ put away Ⓑ drop Ⓒ grab Ⓓ hide

Circle all of the s-blend words in the story and then write the words in the box below.

Grade 3 Phonics and Spelling Workbook   Created by Mrs. Indira Coleby-Demeritte

UNIT 15 S Blends — Page 88

ASSESSMENT

Date: _____   Score: _____

Look at each picture. Say the name quietly to yourself and then fill in the s blends to match each picture.

Picture	Word	Picture	Word
star	___ ar	dog	___ iffed
sweater	___ eater	scarecrow	___ arecrow
snowflake	___ owflake	scale	___ ale
speaker	___ eaker	swing	___ ing
spoon	___ oon	spider	___ ider
swan	___ an	smile	___ ile
sports	___ orts	scarf	___ arf
snail	___ ail	stone	___ one
sky	___ y	skirt	___ irt
skunk	___ unk	slide	___ ide

Grade 3 Phonics and Spelling Workbook   Created by Mrs. Indira Coleby-Demeritte

UNIT 15 S Blends   Page 89

MONDAY — SPELLING PRACTICE

Look at each picture and then write the spelling word that matches it.

(stamp)	(scarecrow)	(spider)
(sweater)	(smile)	(snowflake)
(speaker)	(scorpion)	(scale)

TUESDAY — SPELLING PRACTICE

Classify the spelling words by their S-Blends. Write them in the correct chart below.

SP	SN

SM	SW

Spelling Words

1. smile
2. smart
3. spend
4. sting
5. stream
6. spelling
7. scale
8. smell
9. stamp
10. snowflake
11. sweater
12. swollen
13. special
14. slender
15. sport
16. sniffed
17. spider
18. scarecrow
19. speaker
20. snail

Grade 3 Phonics and Spelling Workbook — Created by Mrs. Indira Coleby-Demeritte

UNIT 15 S Blends

Page 90

WEDNESDAY — SPELLING PRACTICE

Use the word box to write the rhyming word for the words listed below.

smart	spend	slender
speaker	spelling	smile

1. weaker _____
2. while _____
3. blender _____
4. tart _____
5. lend _____
6. telling _____

THURSDAY — SPELLING PRACTICE

Look at the first letter of each word. Write the words in Alphabetical Order. The alphabet chart below will help you.

A B C D E F G H I J K L M N O P Q R S T U V W X Y Z

1. slender
2. swollen
3. special
4. snowflake
5. smell

Spelling Words

1. smile
2. smart
3. spend
4. sting
5. stream
6. spelling
7. scale
8. smell
9. stamp
10. snowflake
11. sweater
12. swollen
13. special
14. slender
15. sport
16. sniffed
17. spider
18. scarecrow
19. speaker
20. snail

UNIT 15 S Blends

Practice the spelling of each word below by writing it in it's column.

smile	spelling	sweater	sniffed	smart

scale	swollen	spider	spend	smell

Grade 3 Phonics and Spelling Workbook — *Created by Mrs. Indira Coleby-Demeritte*

UNIT 15 S Blends

Page 92

Practice the spelling of each word below by writing it in it's column.

special	scarecrow	sting	stamp	slender

speaker	stream	snowflake	sport	snail

Grade 3 Phonics and Spelling Workbook *Created by Mrs. Indira Coleby-Demeritte*

UNIT 16 Final Consonant Blends   Page 93

MONDAY — PHONICS PRACTICE

Use the word box to write the name of each picture and circle the final consonant blend. The first one has been done for you.

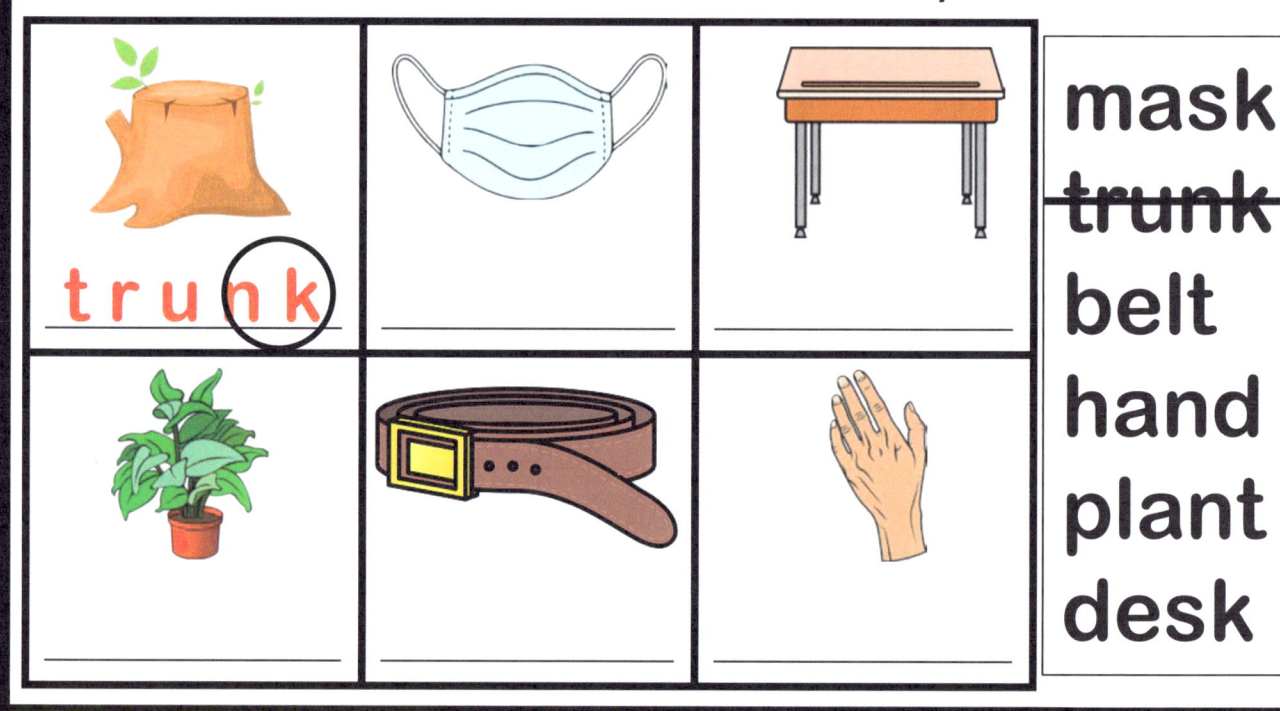

tru(n)k

Word box:
- mask
- ~~trunk~~
- belt
- hand
- plant
- desk

TUESDAY — PHONICS PRACTICE

Look at the word bank. Use the words to fill in the blanks. Then read the story!

| gift | lift | child | cold | felt | quilt |

An Old Quilt

Grandma gave me a birthday _____.
It was an old _____.
Grandma had it since she was a _____.
It was so heavy that I could hardly _____ it!
It _____ nice and soft.
It will keep me warm on _____ nights.

Grade 3 Phonics and Spelling Workbook — Created by Mrs. Indira Coleby-Demeritte

UNIT 16 Final Consonant Blends — Page 94

WEDNESDAY — PHONICS PRACTICE

Look at each picture and use the word box write the final consonant to complete each word.

			Word Box
she__ __	si__ __	gi __ __	st
			lk
			nd
 mi __ __	 ne __ __	 po __ __	nk
			ft
			lf

THURSDAY — PHONICS PRACTICE

Read the story and answer the questions.

The Hulk

The Hulk is green like a beanstalk. He has arms that can bulk out of a silk shirt. The Hulk is strong as an elk. He drinks his milk everyday. When the Hulk talks, everyone runs away.

1. What is the Hulk the color of?
   ....
2. What does the Hulk's arm bulk out from?
   ....
3. What does the Hulk drink everyday?
   ....
4. What is a synonym for elk?
   Ⓐ pig Ⓑ rabbit Ⓒ deer Ⓓ lamb

Circle all of the -lk blend words in the story and then write the words in the box below.

Grade 3 Phonics and Spelling Workbook — Created by Mrs. Indira Coleby-Demeritte

UNIT 16 Final Consonant Blends — Page 95

ASSESSMENT

Date: _____   Score: _____

Say the name for each picture. Use the word box to write the name for each picture. Underline the ending blend.

skunk	mask	blimp	desk	lamp	ring	plant
fist	jump	tusk	stamp	wink	film	east

1. mask
2. fist
3. film
4. desk
5. jump
6. skunk
7. plant
8. tusk
9. blimp
10. ring
11. stamp
12. wink
13. east
14. lamp

Grade 3 Phonics and Spelling Workbook   Created by Mrs. Indira Coleby-Demeritte

UNIT 16 Final Consonant Blends

Page 96

MONDAY — SPELLING PRACTICE

Look at each picture and then write the spelling word that matches it.

TUESDAY — SPELLING PRACTICE

Classify the spelling words by their ending blends. Write them in the correct chart below.

-lf	-ft

-nd	-lt

Spelling Words

1. mask
2. gift
3. kind
4. realm
5. list
6. desk
7. shield
8. sulk
9. belt
10. shelf
11. golf
12. pond
13. grasp
14. scalp
15. breakfast
16. crust
17. knelt
18. round
19. raft
20. drift

Grade 3 Phonics and Spelling Workbook Created by Mrs. Indira Coleby-Demeritte

UNIT 16 Final Consonant Blends — Page 97

WEDNESDAY — SPELLING PRACTICE

Use the word box to write the word that matches each description.

sulk	crust	kind
drift	realm	scalp

1. When you treat someone nice, you are _____.
2. This is another word for a kingdom. _____
3. A sad person does this to show their emotions. _____
4. When your head is itchy, you scratch this. _____
5. When you move from place to place, you _____.
6. Pizzas and pies have this. _____

THURSDAY — SPELLING PRACTICE

Classify the spelling words by their ending blends. Write them in the correct chart below.

-st	-sk

-lm	-sp

Spelling Words

1. mask
2. gift
3. kind
4. realm
5. list
6. desk
7. shield
8. sulk
9. belt
10. shelf
11. golf
12. pond
13. grasp
14. scalp
15. breakfast
16. crust
17. knelt
18. round
19. raft
20. drift

Grade 3 Phonics and Spelling Workbook — Created by Mrs. Indira Coleby-Demeritte

UNIT 16 Final Consonant Blends

Practice the spelling of each word below by writing it in it's column.

mask	gift	kind	realm	list

desk	shield	sulk	belt	shelf

UNIT 16 Final Consonant Blends

Practice the spelling of each word below by writing it in it's column.

golf	pond	grasp	scalp	breakfast

crust	knelt	round	raft	drift

Grade 3 Phonics and Spelling Workbook   *Created by Mrs. Indira Coleby-Demeritte*

UNIT 17 R-Controlled Vowels AR & OR   Page 100

MONDAY — PHONICS PRACTICE

Look at each picture and say it's name to your self. Then color the r-controlled sound you hear for each word.

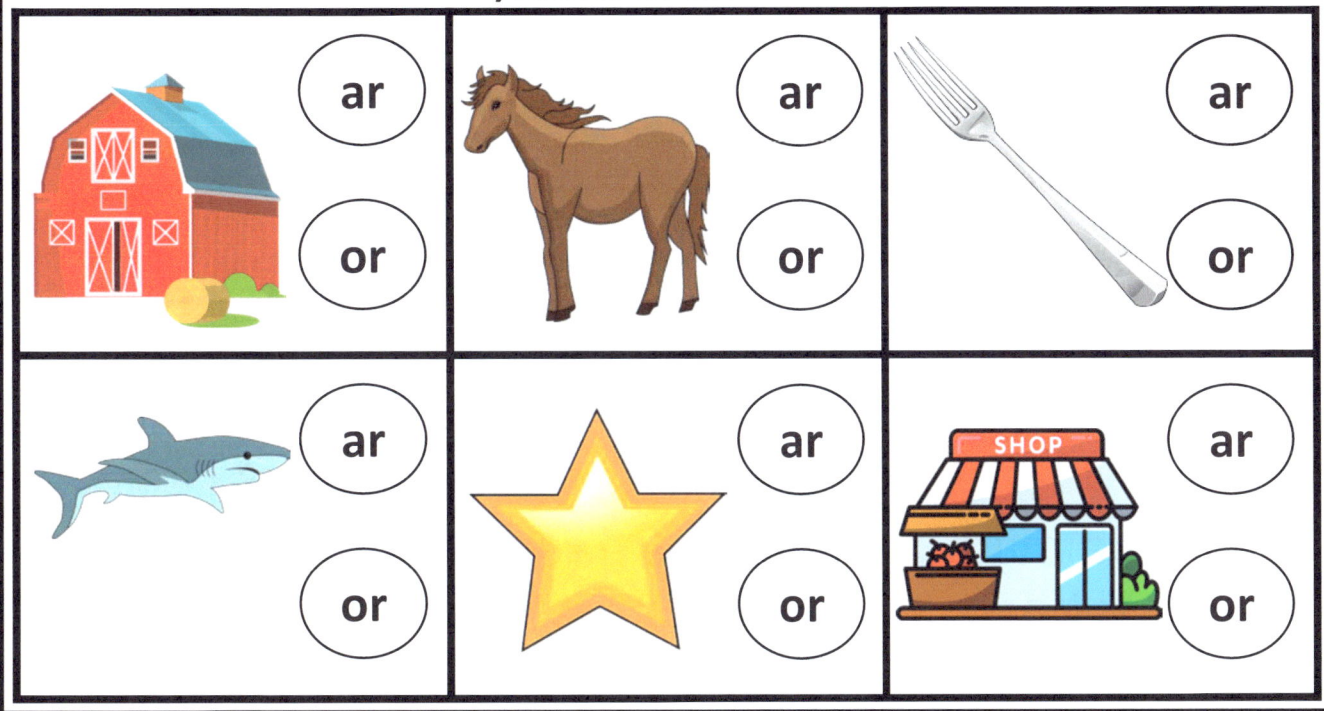

barn	ar / or
horse	ar / or
fork	ar / or
shark	ar / or
star	ar / or
shop (store)	ar / or

TUESDAY — PHONICS PRACTICE

Circle the word that matches the picture. Then write the r-controlled vowel on the lines below.

corn	corn / con
jar	gare / jar
guitar	guitar / guitre
scarf	scarfe / scarf
horn	horn / hone
orange	orange / arange

_____

Grade 3 Phonics and Spelling Workbook   *Created by Mrs. Indira Coleby-Demeritte*

UNIT 17 R-Controlled Vowels AR & OR — Page 101

WEDNESDAY — PHONICS PRACTICE

Use the word box to complete each sentence.

car	art	far
hard	start	part

1. Drew drives a red _____.
2. Brielle likes to paint in _____ class.
3. What time does the game _____?
4. How _____ is it to Grandpa's house?
5. These math problems are really _____!
6. Craig has a small _____ in the school play.

THURSDAY — PHONICS PRACTICE

Read the story and answer the questions.

Chores

Corey had to do his chores on Saturday, before he could go and play sports. He had to help his mom go to the store, work in the garden, feed his horse, and many more. He was never bored. Then, he got to go play. He was so tired at night that he would really snore.

1. What did Corey have to do first?
_____

2. Where did Corey go with his mom on Saturday?
_____

3. What did Corey do at night, because he was so tired?
_____

4. What is a synonym for <u>chore</u>?
Ⓐ play Ⓑ away Ⓒ task Ⓓ take

Circle all of the <u>or</u> words in the story and then write the words in the box below.

Grade 3 Phonics and Spelling Workbook — Created by Mrs. Indira Coleby-Demeritte

UNIT 17 R-Controlled Vowels AR & OR   Page 102

ASSESSMENT

Date: _____   Score: _____

Use the word box to write an <u>ar</u> word to complete each sentence.

art	arm	car	dark
farm	park	shark	star

1. Meg is driving her __ __ __ .

2. She saw rows of corn when she drove by the __ __ __ __ .

3. Last night we saw a bright __ __ __ __ in the sky.

4. Dan took his dog for a walk in the __ __ __ __ .

5. Thank goodness you didn't break your __ __ __ when you fell.

6. In __ __ __ class, I painted a picture of a snake.

7. Please keep the lights on because I am afraid of the __ __ __ __ .

8. A __ __ __ __ __ with big teeth swam in the ocean.

Grade 3 Phonics and Spelling Workbook   Created by Mrs. Indira Coleby-Demeritte

UNIT 17 R-Controlled Vowels AR & OR — Page 103

MONDAY — SPELLING PRACTICE

Look at each picture and then write the spelling word that matches it.

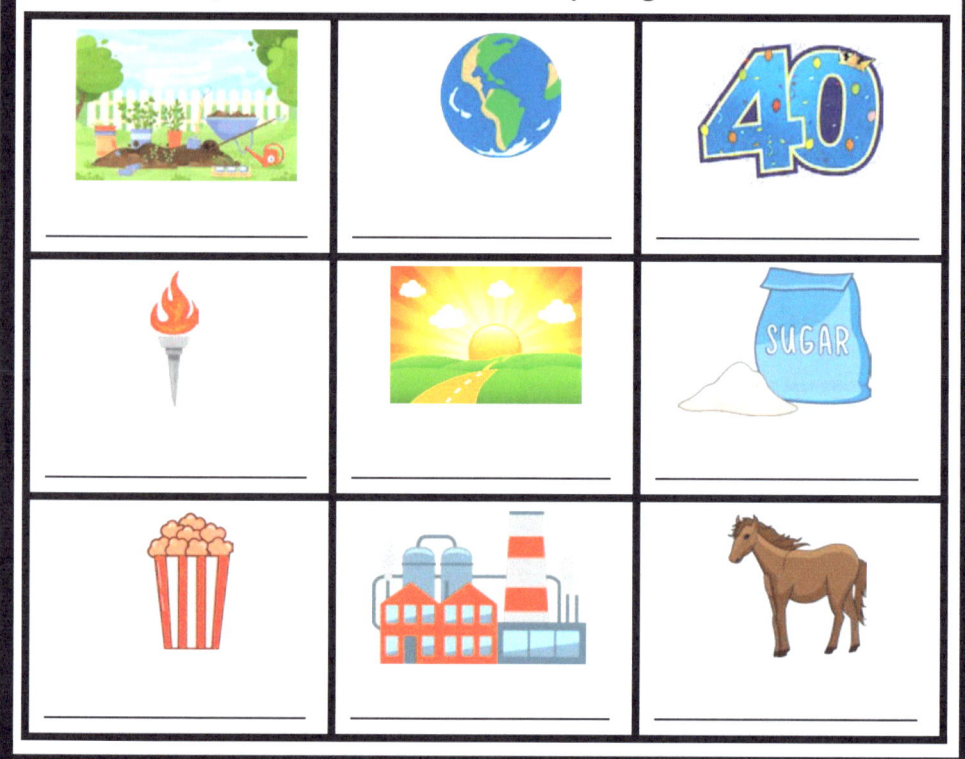

(garden) _____	(world) _____	(forty) _____
(torch) _____	(morning) _____	(sugar) _____
(popcorn) _____	(factory) _____	(horse) _____

TUESDAY — SPELLING PRACTICE

Classify the spelling words by their r-controlled sound. Write them in the correct chart below.

AR	OR

Spelling Words

1. factory
2. sugar
3. sparkling
4. popcorn
5. honor
6. workbook
7. morning
8. favorite
9. world
10. order
11. garden
12. partied
13. large
14. torch
15. worried
16. startled
17. guitar
18. bored
19. forty
20. horse

Grade 3 Phonics and Spelling Workbook Created by Mrs. Indira Coleby-Demeritte

UNIT 17 R-Controlled Vowels AR & OR   Page 104

WEDNESDAY — SPELLING PRACTICE

Use the word box to write a synonym for the words listed below.

order	world	torch
sweets	large	worried

1. sugar_____
2. sequence_____
3. concerned_____
4. light_____
5. enormous_____
6. globe_____

THURSDAY — SPELLING PRACTICE

Divide each word below into syllables.

1. popcorn _____
2. workbook_____
3. garden _____
4. guitar _____
5. sparkling _____
6. favorite _____
7. order _____
8. factory_____

Spelling Words

1. factory
2. sugar
3. sparkling
4. popcorn
5. honor
6. workbook
7. morning
8. favorite
9. world
10. order
11. garden
12. partied
13. large
14. torch
15. worried
16. startled
17. guitar
18. bored
19. forty
20. horse

Grade 3 Phonics and Spelling Workbook   Created by Mrs. Indira Coleby-Demeritte

UNIT 17 R-Controlled Vowels AR & OR   Page 105

Practice the spelling of each word below by writing it in it's column.

factory	sugar	sparkling	popcorn	honor

workbook	morning	favorite	world	order

Grade 3 Phonics and Spelling Workbook   *Created by Mrs. Indira Coleby-Demeritte*

UNIT 17 R-Controlled Vowels AR & OR   Page 106

Practice the spelling of each word below by writing it in it's column.

garden	partied	large	torch	worried

startled	guitar	bored	forty	horse

Grade 3 Phonics and Spelling Workbook   *Created by Mrs. Indira Coleby-Demeritte*

UNIT 18 R-Controlled Vowels ER, IR & UR Page 107

MONDAY — PHONICS PRACTICE

Say the name of each picture. Circle the er, ir or ur in each name.

feather	bird	circus
nurse	tiger	turkey

TUESDAY — PHONICS PRACTICE

Circle the word that matches the picture. Then write the r-controlled vowel on the lines below.

girms / germs	purse / perse	grl / girl
hurt / hert	skert / skirt	hammor / hammer

Grade 3 Phonics and Spelling Workbook Created by Mrs. Indira Coleby-Demeritte

UNIT 18 R-Controlled Vowels ER, IR & UR   Page 108

WEDNESDAY — PHONICS PRACTICE

Look at the word bank. Use the words to fill in the blanks. Then read the story!

| her | bird | chirp | girl | hurt | nurse |

Irma and the Bird

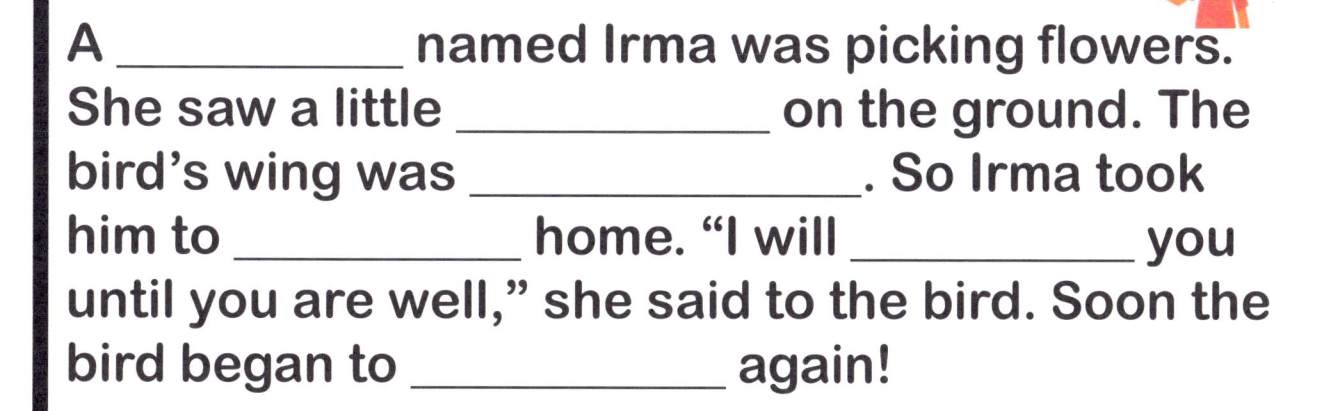

A _____ named Irma was picking flowers. She saw a little _____ on the ground. The bird's wing was _____. So Irma took him to _____ home. "I will _____ you until you are well," she said to the bird. Soon the bird began to _____ again!

THURSDAY — PHONICS PRACTICE

Read the story and answer the questions.

The Surfer

Jen likes to surf at the beach. She is good and can turn around on her board in the water. Jen always puts on her sunscreen, so she will not burn in the sun. One Thursday, she got hurt falling off her board, but she returned on Saturday to surf some more.

1. What does Jen like to do?
   _____

2. What does Jen always put on before going in the sun?
   _____

3. What happened to Jen on Thursday?
   _____

4. What is a synonym for <u>return</u>?
   Ⓐ left Ⓑ done Ⓒ leave Ⓓ go back

Circle all of the <u>ur</u> words in the story and then write the words in the box below.

Grade 3 Phonics and Spelling Workbook — Created by Mrs. Indira Coleby-Demeritte

UNIT 18 R-Controlled Vowels ER, IR & UR Page 109

ASSESSMENT

Date: _____   Score: _____

Say the name of each picture. Use the word box to write it's name. Then sort the words in the correct columns below.

star	horse	river	thirteen	tractor	turkey
nurse	corn	bird	shark	letter	yarn

1. _____
2. _____
3. _____
4. _____
5. _____
6. _____
7. _____
8. _____
9. _____
10. _____
11. _____
12. _____

AR	ER	IR	OR	UR

Grade 3 Phonics and Spelling Workbook   Created by Mrs. Indira Coleby-Demeritte

UNIT 18 R-Controlled Vowels ER, IR & UR Page 110

MONDAY — SPELLING PRACTICE

Look at each picture and then write the spelling word that matches it.

_____	_____	_____
_____	_____	_____
_____	_____	_____

TUESDAY — SPELLING PRACTICE

Unscramble the spelling word. The first letter is underlined.

1. up<u>c</u>mtreo _____
1. iwl<u>t</u>r _____
2. staore<u>t</u> _____
3. virece<u>s</u> _____
4. n<u>r</u>true _____
5. nsre<u>a</u>w _____
6. dyi<u>b</u>rhta _____
7. th<u>t</u>yri _____
8. yaut<u>S</u>adr _____

Spelling Words

1. birthday
2. yesterday
3. blender
4. toaster
5. thunderstorm
6. squirrel
7. answer
8. letter
9. girl
10. service
11. computer
12. turtle
13. purple
14. nurse
15. firstly
16. twirl
17. Saturday
18. thirty
19. turkey
20. return

Grade 3 Phonics and Spelling Workbook — Created by Mrs. Indira Coleby-Demeritte

UNIT 18 R-Controlled Vowels ER, IR & UR Page 111

WEDNESDAY — SPELLING PRACTICE

Use your spelling list to sort the spelling words. Some words may be used on both groups.

ER	IR

UR	

THURSDAY — SPELLING PRACTICE

Circle the r-controlled vowel for each spelling word and then write in on the lines to complete each word.

Squ __ __ rel	er	ir
Thund __ __ storm	er	ur
Answ __ __	ir	er
F __ __ stly	ir	ur
Ret __ __ n	er	ur
Yest __ __ day	er	ir
B __ __ thday	ir	ur
Lett __ __	ur	er

Spelling Words

1. birthday
2. yesterday
3. blender
4. toaster
5. thunderstorm
6. squirrel
7. answer
8. letter
9. girl
10. service
11. computer
12. turtle
13. purple
14. nurse
15. firstly
16. twirl
17. Saturday
18. thirty
19. turkey
20. return

Grade 3 Phonics and Spelling Workbook *Created by Mrs. Indira Coleby-Demeritte*

UNIT 18 R-Controlled Vowels ER, IR & UR   Page 112

Practice the spelling of each word below by writing it in it's column.

birthday	yesterday	blender	toaster	thunderstorm

squirrel	answer	letter	girl	service

Grade 3 Phonics and Spelling Workbook   *Created by Mrs. Indira Coleby-Demeritte*

UNIT 18 R-Controlled Vowels ER, IR & UR Page 113

Practice the spelling of each word below by writing it in it's column.

computer	turtle	purple	nurse	firstly

twirl	Saturday	thirty	turkey	return

Grade 3 Phonics and Spelling Workbook — *Created by Mrs. Indira Coleby-Demeritte*

UNIT 19 Compound Words

Page 114

MONDAY — PHONICS PRACTICE

Look at each picture and say its name quietly to yourself. Then draw lines to make compound words.

TUESDAY — PHONICS PRACTICE

Look at each picture and then use the word box to make compound words.

1.  🐕 + 🏠 = _____ 
2.  🌊 + 🐚 = _____ 
3.  🫖 + 🍲 = _____ 
4.  ☁️🌧 + 🎀 = _____ 
5. 🦶 + 🏀 = _____

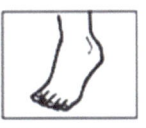

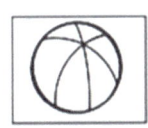

Word Box
house
ball
pot
dog
tea
shell
foot
bow
rain
sea

Grade 3 Phonics and Spelling Workbook *Created by Mrs. Indira Coleby-Demeritte*

UNIT 19 Compound Words — Page 115

WEDNESDAY — PHONICS PRACTICE

Use the word box to match each compound word to its clue.

backpack	bathtub	outside	shoelace
countertop	treetop	seashell	overhead

1. The top of a tree _____
2. The opposite of inside _____
3. A shell near the sea _____
4. A tub for a bath _____
5. The top of the counter _____
6. A bag on your back _____
7. Over your head _____
8. A lace for a shoe _____

THURSDAY — PHONICS PRACTICE

Read the story and circle all of the compound words. Then write them on the lines.

Samson

It was sunrise on Sunday. Samson saw the sunshine above the treetop. He jumped up and went outside. He saw a beehive, then he found a seashell in the sandbox. Samson had fun and then went inside for pancakes.

Circle all of the <u>Compound</u> words in the story and then write them down below.

1. _____ 5. _____
2. _____ 6. _____
3. _____ 7. _____
4. _____ 8. _____

There are _____ compound words!

Grade 3 Phonics and Spelling Workbook
Created by Mrs. Indira Coleby-Demeritte

UNIT 19 Compound Words Page 116

ASSESSMENT

Date: _____   Score: _____

Choose two words in each sentence to put together into a compound word to illustrate the picture.

1. A house for a dog is a _____ .

2. A man made out of snow is a _____.

3. A shell from the sea is a _____ .

4. A bird that is blue is a _____ .

5. A hive for a bee is a _____ .

6. A bell for a door is a _____ .

7. A room for a bed is a _____ .

8. A pot for tea is a _____ .

Grade 3 Phonics and Spelling Workbook   Created by Mrs. Indira Coleby-Demeritte

UNIT 19 Compound Words

Page 117

MONDAY — SPELLING PRACTICE

Look at each picture and then write the spelling word that matches it.

TUESDAY — SPELLING PRACTICE

Use your spelling list to classify the words by how many syllables they have.

2 Syllables	3 Syllables

Spelling Words

1. teapot
2. headache
3. watermelon
4. countertop
5. sunshine
6. necktie
7. shoelace
8. seashell
9. notebook
10. peanuts
11. paintbrush
12. raincoat
13. beehive
14. treetop
15. rattlesnake
16. outside
17. pancake
18. waterfall
19. dustpan
20. spaceship

Grade 3 Phonics and Spelling Workbook *Created by Mrs. Indira Coleby-Demeritte*

UNIT 19 Compound Words

WEDNESDAY — SPELLING PRACTICE

Use your spelling list to fill in the missing word from each compound. Then write the full compound word on the line.

1. _____ + book = _____
2. tree + _____ = _____
3. _____ + snake = _____
4. _____ + side = _____
5. head + _____ = _____
6. _____ + fall = _____
7. _____ + ship = _____
8. _____ + top = _____
9. sun + _____ = _____
10. water + _____ = _____

THURSDAY — SPELLING PRACTICE

Look at the first letter of each word. Write the words in Alphabetical Order. The alphabet chart below will help you.

A B C D E F G H I J K L M N O P Q R S T U V W X Y Z

1. paintbrush
2. spaceship
3. raincoat
4. sunshine
5. headache

Spelling Words

1. teapot
2. headache
3. watermelon
4. countertop
5. sunshine
6. necktie
7. shoelace
8. seashell
9. notebook
10. peanuts
11. paintbrush
12. raincoat
13. beehive
14. treetop
15. rattlesnake
16. outside
17. pancake
18. waterfall
19. dustpan
20. spaceship

Grade 3 Phonics and Spelling Workbook Created by Mrs. Indira Coleby-Demeritte

UNIT 19 Compound Words

Practice the spelling of each word below by writing it in it's column.

teapot	headache	watermelon	countertop	sunshine

necktie	shoelace	seashell	notebook	peanuts

UNIT 19 Compound Words — Page 120

Practice the spelling of each word below by writing it in it's column.

paintbrush	raincoat	beehive	treetop	rattlesnake

outside	pancake	waterfall	dustpan	spaceship

Grade 3 Phonics and Spelling Workbook — Created by Mrs. Indira Coleby-Demeritte

UNIT 20 Diphthongs Oi, Oy, Ou, Ow — Page 121

MONDAY — PHONICS PRACTICE

Say the name of each picture. Circle the <u>ou</u> or <u>ow</u> in each name.

- c o w
- h o u s e 
- c r o w d 
- c l o u d
- b l o u s e 
- c l o w n 

TUESDAY — PHONICS PRACTICE

Circle the word that matches the picture. Then write the diphthong on the lines below.

- coin / coyn
- soil / soyl 
- toy / toi 
- boi / boy 
- oister / oyster 
- toilet / toylet 

Grade 3 Phonics and Spelling Workbook — Created by Mrs. Indira Coleby-Demeritte

UNIT 20 Diphthongs Oi, Oy, Ou, Ow   Page 122

WEDNESDAY — PHONICS PRACTICE

Use the word box to complete each sentence.

points	soil	cowboys	join
enjoy	noise	boiled	coiled

1. We _____ going on long rides on horses.
2. We make believe we are cowgirls and _____.
3. Once we heard a snake's loud _____.
4. We saw a snake in the dirt, or _____.
5. The snake was _____, so we rode away.
6. Another time, we rode to a place where two streams _____, or come together.
7. We camped near a big rock with five _____ on it.
8. Then we _____ water over the hot campfire.

THURSDAY — PHONICS PRACTICE

Read the story and answer the questions.

Before Town

One summer day, Mrs. Brown wanted to go for a walk around town. Before she left, she had to water her flowers; milk her cows; hang her towels out to dry; feed her owl; and take a shower. "Wow!" said Mrs. Brown. "Now, I can go to town."

1. Who wanted to go for a walk?
   _____
2. What did Mrs. Brown have to hang?
   _____
3. What did Mrs. Brown have to feed?
   _____
4. What is a synonym for town?
   Ⓐ sea Ⓑ city Ⓒ farm Ⓓ pond

Circle all of the ow words in the story and then write the words in the box below.

Grade 3 Phonics and Spelling Workbook   Created by Mrs. Indira Coleby-Demeritte

UNIT 20 Diphthongs Oi, Oy, Ou, Ow

ASSESSMENT

Date: _____   Score: _____

Write an ow, or ou word to complete each sentence below.
There's a clue to help you after each sentence.

1. Have you seen my __ __ __ __ __ crayon? (b r - - n)

2. There is one, fluffy __ __ __ __ __ in the sky. (c l - - d)

3. I need to pick up some __ __ __ __ __ at the grocery store. (f l - - r)

4. Please keep your __ __ __ __ __ closed when you chew. (m - - t h)

5. I built a __ __ __ __ __ with my Lego blocks. (t - - e r)

6. There's a __ __ __ in the farmer's field. (c - -)

7. My cat won't come __ __ __ __ from that tree branch. (d - - n)

8. She was as quiet as a __ __ __ __ __. (m - - s e)

Grade 3 Phonics and Spelling Workbook   *Created by Mrs. Indira Coleby-Demeritte*

UNIT 20 Diphthongs Oi, Oy, Ou, Ow   Page 124

MONDAY — SPELLING PRACTICE

Look at each picture and then write the spelling word that matches it.

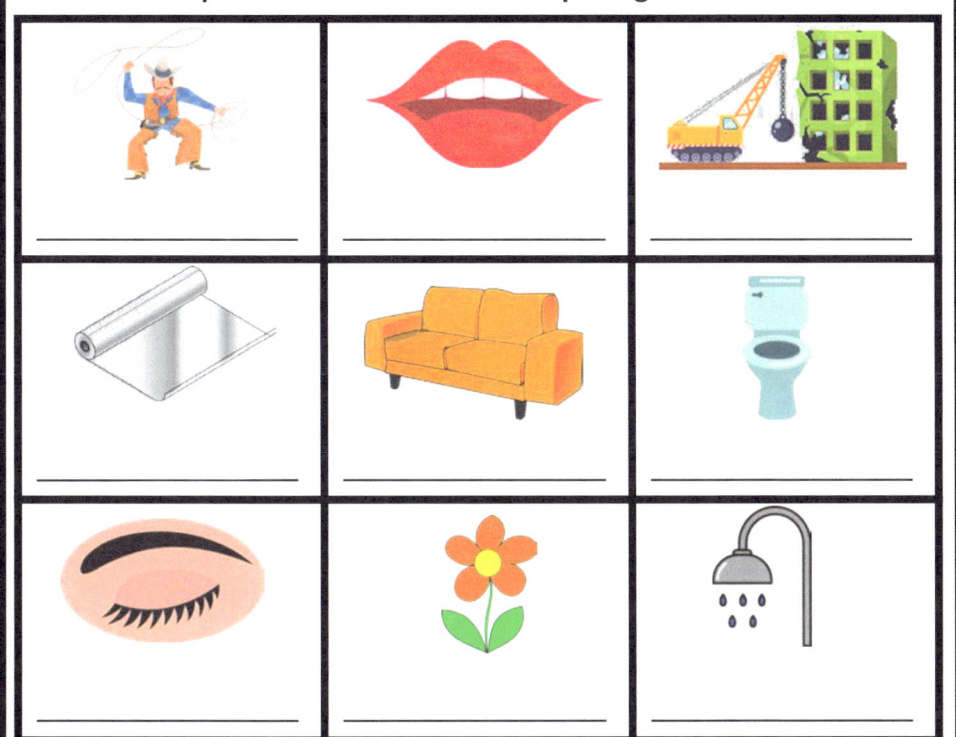

(cowboy) _____	(mouth) _____	(destroy) _____
(foil) _____	(couch) _____	(toilet) _____
(eyebrow) _____	(flower) _____	(shower) _____

TUESDAY — SPELLING PRACTICE

Use your spelling list to classify the words in the columns below.
Add 2 new words under the OY columns.

Oi	Oy
	Add a word
	Add a word

Spelling Words

1. choice
2. enjoy
3. rejoice
4. loudest
5. foil
6. shout
7. couch
8. flower
9. toilet
10. point
11. noun
12. eyebrow
13. moisture
14. destroy
15. shower
16. power
17. downtown
18. cowboy
19. mouth
20. found

Grade 3 Phonics and Spelling Workbook   *Created by Mrs. Indira Coleby-Demeritte*

UNIT 20 Diphthongs Oi, Oy, Ou, Ow

Page 125

WEDNESDAY — SPELLING PRACTICE

Use the word box to write a rhyming word for the words listed below.

flower	choice	foil
found	noun	shout

1. town_____
2. power_____
3. oil_____
4. route_____
5. pound_____
6. voice _____

THURSDAY — SPELLING PRACTICE

Use your spelling list to classify the words in the columns below.

Ou	Ow

Spelling Words

1. choice
2. enjoy
3. rejoice
4. loudest
5. foil
6. shout
7. couch
8. flower
9. toilet
10. point
11. noun
12. eyebrow
13. moisture
14. destroy
15. shower
16. power
17. downtown
18. cowboy
19. mouth
20. found

Grade 3 Phonics and Spelling Workbook Created by Mrs. Indira Coleby-Demeritte

UNIT 20 Diphthongs Oi, Oy, Ou, Ow

Practice the spelling of each word below by writing it in it's column.

choice	enjoy	rejoice	loudest	foil

shout	couch	flower	toilet	point

UNIT 20 Diphthongs Oi, Oy, Ou, Ow

Practice the spelling of each word below by writing it in it's column.

noun	eyebrow	moisture	destroy	shower

power	downtown	cowboy	mouth	found

Grade 3 Phonics and Spelling Workbook   *Created by Mrs. Indira Coleby-Demeritte*

UNIT 21 Diphthongs Au, Aw, Ew, Oo — Page 128

MONDAY — PHONICS PRACTICE

Circle the pictures that have the au/aw sound.

TUESDAY — PHONICS PRACTICE

Use the word box to help you complete each sentence below.

| threw | zooms | boots | stool |

This girl wears _____.

Julian _____ to the moon.

Louis is on the _____.

Eva _____ the ball.

Grade 3 Phonics and Spelling Workbook *Created by Mrs. Indira Coleby-Demeritte*

UNIT 21 Diphthongs Au, Aw, Ew, Oo Page 129

WEDNESDAY — PHONICS PRACTICE

Look at each picture and say it's name to your self. Then color the diphthong sound you hear for each word.

hawk	aw / ew
yawning girl	aw / oo
stump roots	au / oo
screw	au / ew
moon	aw / oo
boy writing	aw / oo

THURSDAY — PHONICS PRACTICE

Look at the word bank. Use the words to fill in the blanks. Then read the story!

| all | always | dawn | draw | Paul | taught |

Draw A Picture

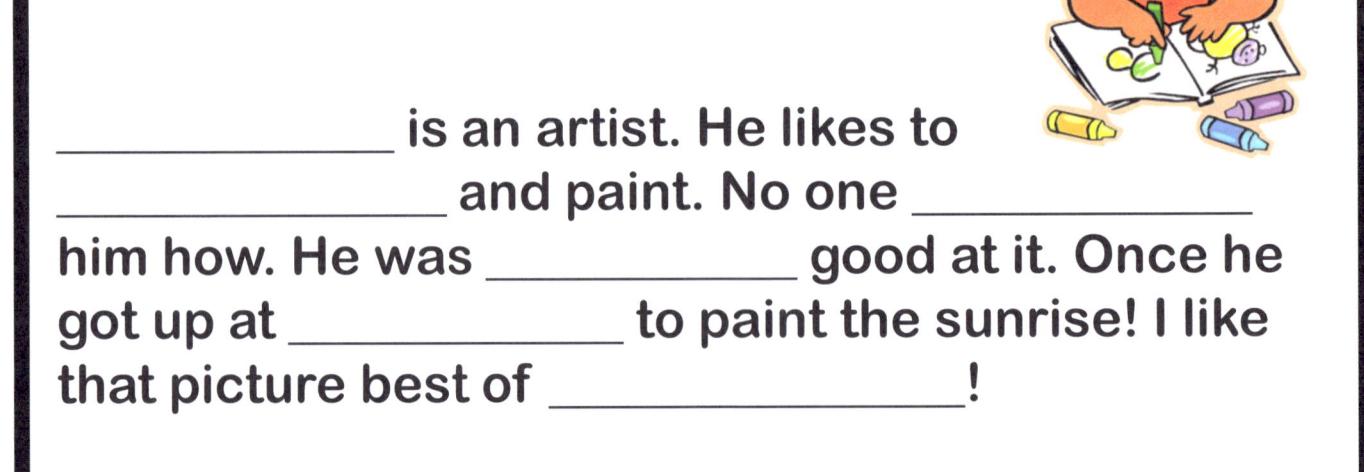

_____ is an artist. He likes to _____ and paint. No one _____ him how. He was _____ good at it. Once he got up at _____ to paint the sunrise! I like that picture best of _____!

Grade 3 Phonics and Spelling Workbook   Created by Mrs. Indira Coleby-Demeritte

UNIT 21 Diphthongs Au, Aw, Ew, Oo — Page 130

ASSESSMENT

Date: _____   Score: _____

Look at each picture, then fill in the blanks to complete the word by writing Au, or Aw.

1. S__ __ cer

2. S __ __

3. L__ __ ndry

4. Cr __ __ fish

5. Dr __ __ ing

6. S __ __ ce

Look at each picture and <u>circle</u> the diphthong you hear in each word.

1.   Ew   au

2.   Ew   au

3.   Aw   oo

4.   Aw   oo

Grade 3 Phonics and Spelling Workbook   Created by Mrs. Indira Coleby-Demeritte

UNIT 21 Diphthongs Au, Aw, Ew, Oo

Page 131

MONDAY — SPELLING PRACTICE

Look at each picture and then write the spelling word that matches it.

TUESDAY — SPELLING PRACTICE

Use your spelling list to classify the words in the columns below.

Au	Aw

Spelling Words

1. awesome
2. laundry
3. screw
4. school
5. August
6. sauce
7. root
8. balloon
9. crawfish
10. because
11. goose
12. cashew
13. saw
14. saucer
15. threw
16. curfew
17. awful
18. drawing
19. smooth
20. nephew

Grade 3 Phonics and Spelling Workbook — *Created by Mrs. Indira Coleby-Demeritte*

UNIT 21 Diphthongs Au, Aw, Ew, Oo

WEDNESDAY — SPELLING PRACTICE

Look at the first letter of each word. Write the words in Alphabetical Order. The alphabet chart below will help you.

A B C D E F G H I J K L M N O P Q R S T U V W X Y Z

1. laundry
2. awesome
3. saucer
4. balloon
5. crawfish
6. because

THURSDAY — SPELLING PRACTICE

Use your spelling list to classify the words in the columns below.

Oo	Ew

Spelling Words

1. awesome
2. laundry
3. screw
4. school
5. August
6. sauce
7. root
8. balloon
9. crawfish
10. because
11. goose
12. cashew
13. saw
14. saucer
15. threw
16. curfew
17. awful
18. drawing
19. smooth
20. nephew

Grade 3 Phonics and Spelling Workbook   Created by Mrs. Indira Coleby-Demeritte

UNIT 21 Diphthongs Au, Aw, Ew, Oo

Practice the spelling of each word below by writing it in it's column.

awesome	laundry	screw	school	August

sauce	root	balloon	crawfish	because

UNIT 21 Diphthongs Au, Aw, Ew, Oo

Practice the spelling of each word below by writing it in it's column.

goose	cashew	saw	saucer	threw

curfew	awful	drawing	smooth	nephew

Grade 3 Phonics and Spelling Workbook — *Created by Mrs. Indira Coleby-Demeritte*

UNIT 22 Vowel Pairs Ai, Ea, Ie, Oa, Ue — Page 135

MONDAY — PHONICS PRACTICE

The vowel pair ie sometimes makes the Long I sound or it can make the Long E sound. Look at each picture and say its name. Then circle whether the word has the long I or long e sound.

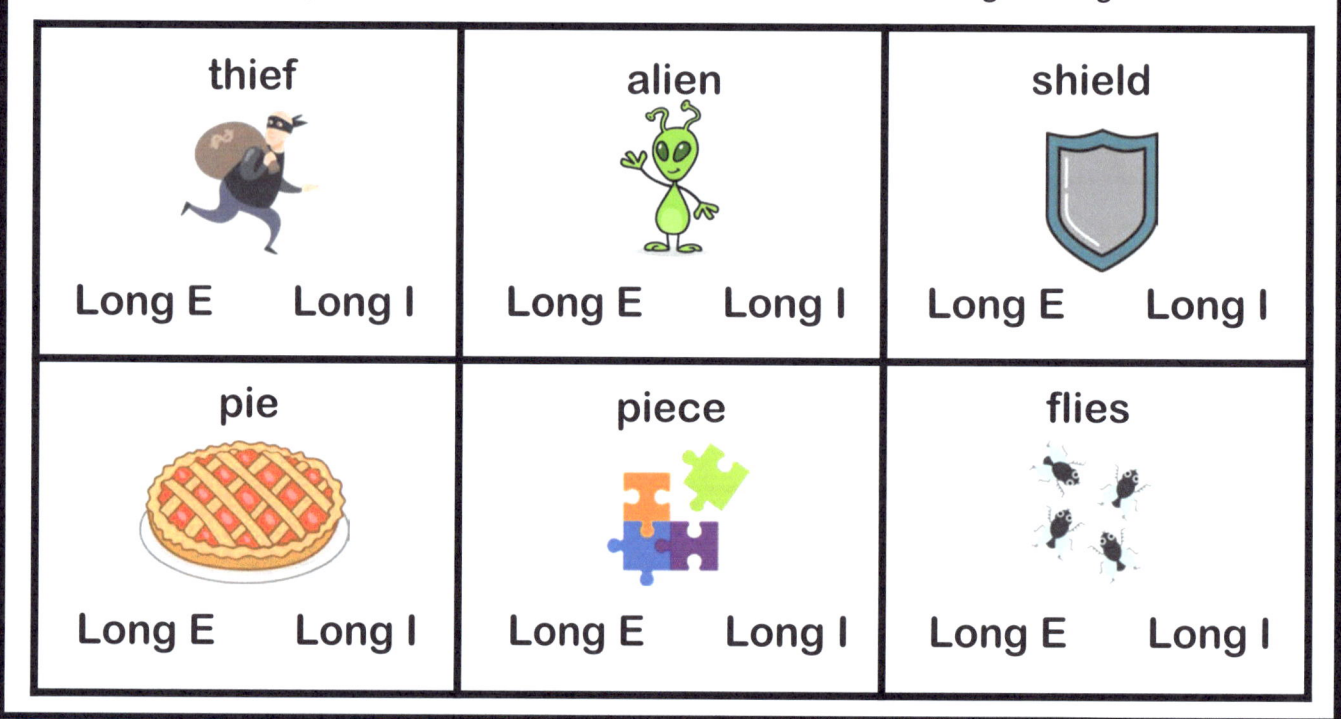

thief	alien	shield
Long E Long I	Long E Long I	Long E Long I
pie	**piece**	**flies**
Long E Long I	Long E Long I	Long E Long I

TUESDAY — PHONICS PRACTICE

The long vowel U makes 2 sounds. It says its name and it can also sounds like oo. Look at each word below. Color the words that make the **u sound red** and the words that make the **oo sound blue**.

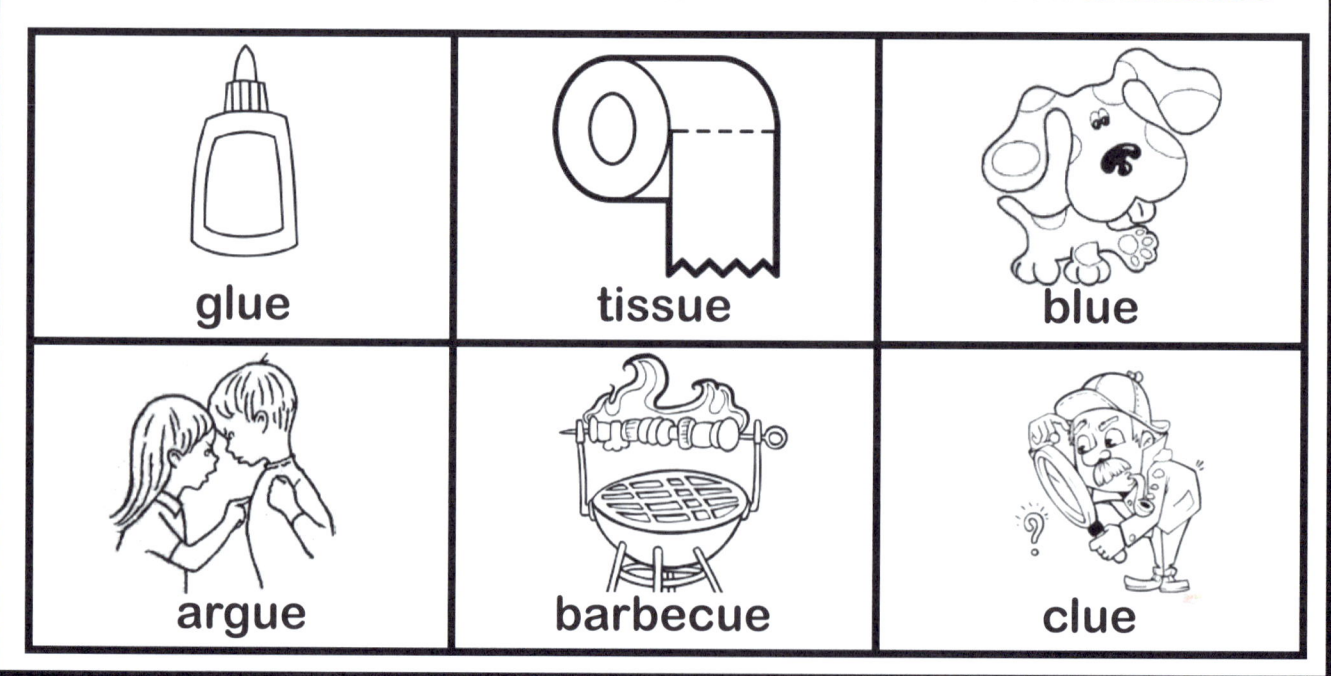

glue	tissue	blue
argue	**barbecue**	**clue**

Grade 3 Phonics and Spelling Workbook — Created by Mrs. Indira Coleby-Demeritte

UNIT 22 Vowel Pairs Ai, Ea, Ie, Oa, Ue — Page 136

WEDNESDAY — PHONICS PRACTICE

The vowel pair **ea** can make 2 sounds. Sometimes it makes the <u>Short E</u> sound like in bread. Sometimes it makes the <u>Long E</u> sound like in teach. Look at the pictures below. Say the name of the first picture in each row, then circle the picture in the row that has the same E sound.

Word 1	Word 2	Word 3	Word 4
beach	weather	bread	bean
head	beak	breath	meat
feather	tea	leaf	spread
peanut	measure	breakfast	seal

THURSDAY — PHONICS PRACTICE

Look at each picture and say its name to yourself. Fill in **oa** or **ai** to complete each spelling.

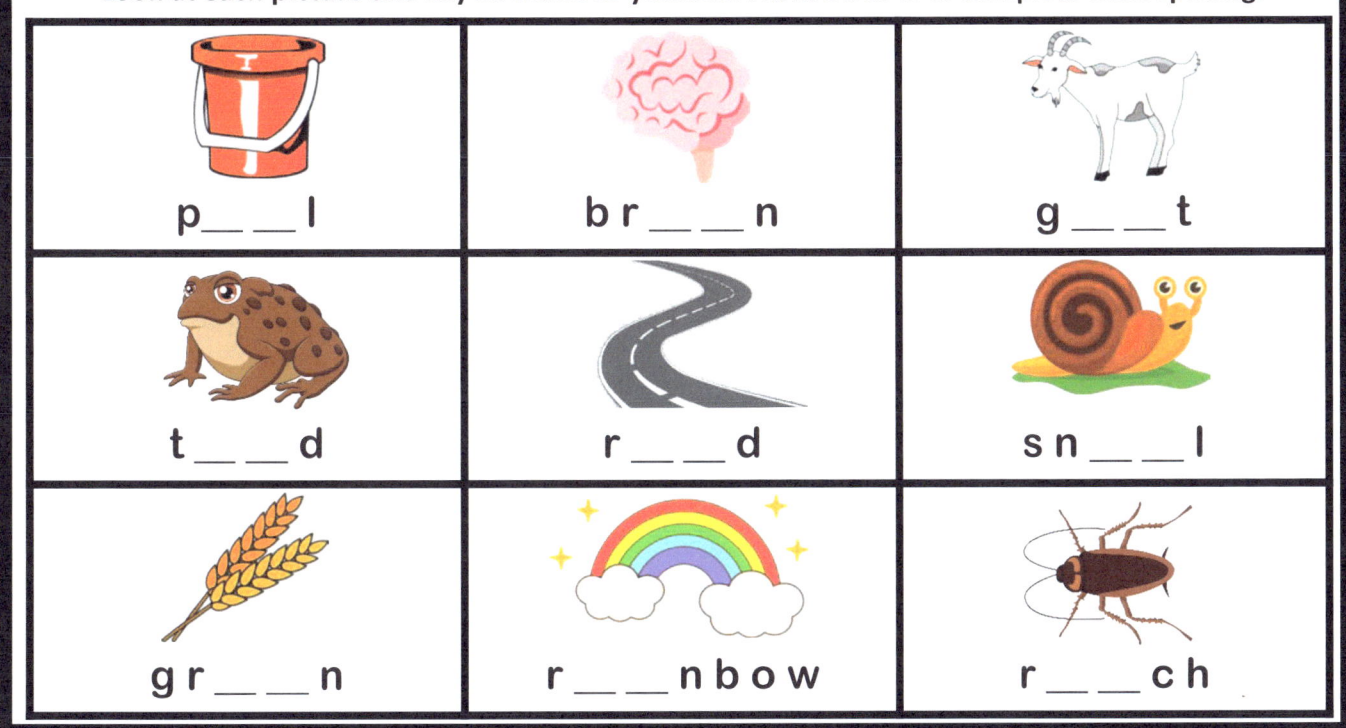

p _ _ l	b r _ _ n	g _ _ t
t _ _ d	r _ _ d	s n _ _ l
g r _ _ n	r _ _ n b o w	r _ _ c h

Grade 3 Phonics and Spelling Workbook   *Created by Mrs. Indira Coleby-Demeritte*

UNIT 22 Vowel Pairs Ai, Ea, Ie, Oa, Ue — Page 137

ASSESSMENT

Date: _____   Score: _____

Draw a line to match the vowel pair with the picture. Then write in the vowel pair to complete each word.

m _ _ t   •   • ai

tiss _ _   •   • ea

s _ _ l   •   • ie

t _ _   •   • oa

gl _ _   •   • ue

b _ _ ch   •   • ue

g _ _ t   •   • ea

Grade 3 Phonics and Spelling Workbook   *Created by Mrs. Indira Coleby-Demeritte*

UNIT 22 Vowel Pairs Ai, Ea, Ie, Oa, Ue — Page 138

MONDAY — SPELLING PRACTICE

Look at each picture and then write the spelling word that matches it.

TUESDAY — SPELLING PRACTICE

Use your spelling list to classify the words in the columns below.

ea	oa	ai

Spelling Words

1. eagle
2. floating
3. statue
4. charcoal
5. peach
6. field
7. cruel
8. oatmeal
9. throat
10. achieve
11. value
12. chain
13. coach
14. believe
15. venue
16. again
17. weakness
18. movie
19. brain
20. complain

Grade 3 Phonics and Spelling Workbook — Created by Mrs. Indira Coleby-Demeritte

UNIT 22 Vowel Pairs Ai, Ea, Ie, Oa, Ue — Page 139

WEDNESDAY — SPELLING PRACTICE

Use the word box to write a rhyming word for the words listed below.

field	peach	throat
achieve	brain	coach

1. roach _____
2. beach _____
3. shield _____
4. chain _____
5. believe _____
6. boat _____

THURSDAY — SPELLING PRACTICE

Use your spelling list to classify the words in the columns below.

ie	ue

Spelling Words

1. eagle
2. floating
3. statue
4. charcoal
5. peach
6. field
7. cruel
8. oatmeal
9. throat
10. achieve
11. value
12. chain
13. coach
14. believe
15. venue
16. again
17. weakness
18. movie
19. brain
20. complain

Grade 3 Phonics and Spelling Workbook
Created by Mrs. Indira Coleby-Demeritte

UNIT 22 Vowel Pairs Ai, Ea, Ie, Oa, Ue — Page 140

Practice the spelling of each word below by writing it in it's column.

eagle	floating	statue	charcoal	peach

field	cruel	oatmeal	throat	achieve

Grade 3 Phonics and Spelling Workbook — *Created by Mrs. Indira Coleby-Demeritte*

UNIT 22 Vowel Pairs Ai, Ea, Ie, Oa, Ue

Practice the spelling of each word below by writing it in it's column.

value	chain	coach	believe	venue

again	weakness	movie	brain	complain

UNIT 23 Digraphs CH, SH, WH, TH — Page 142

MONDAY — PHONICS PRACTICE

Look at each picture and say it's name to your self. Then color the consonant digraph sound you hear for each word.

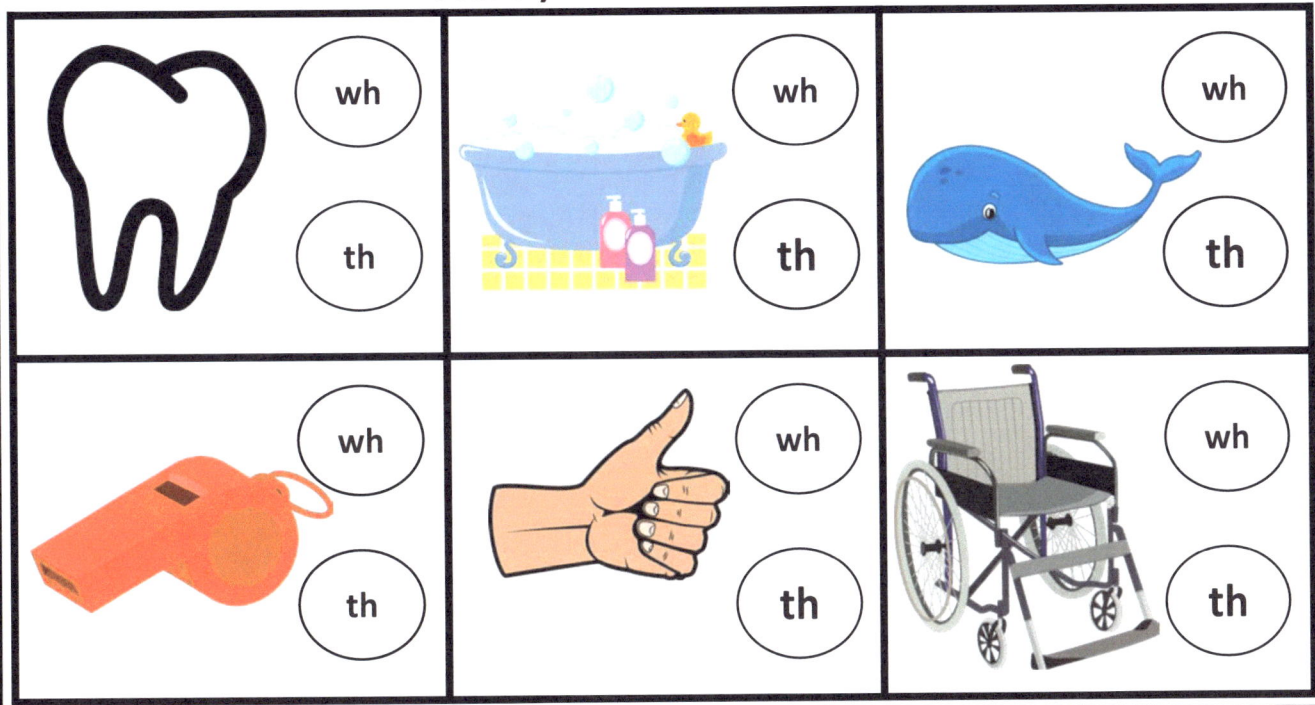

tooth	wh / th
bath	wh / th
whale	wh / th
whistle	wh / th
thumb	wh / th
wheelchair	wh / th

TUESDAY — PHONICS PRACTICE

Look at each picture and say its name quietly to yourself. Circle the correct spelling and then write the consonant digraph on the lines below.

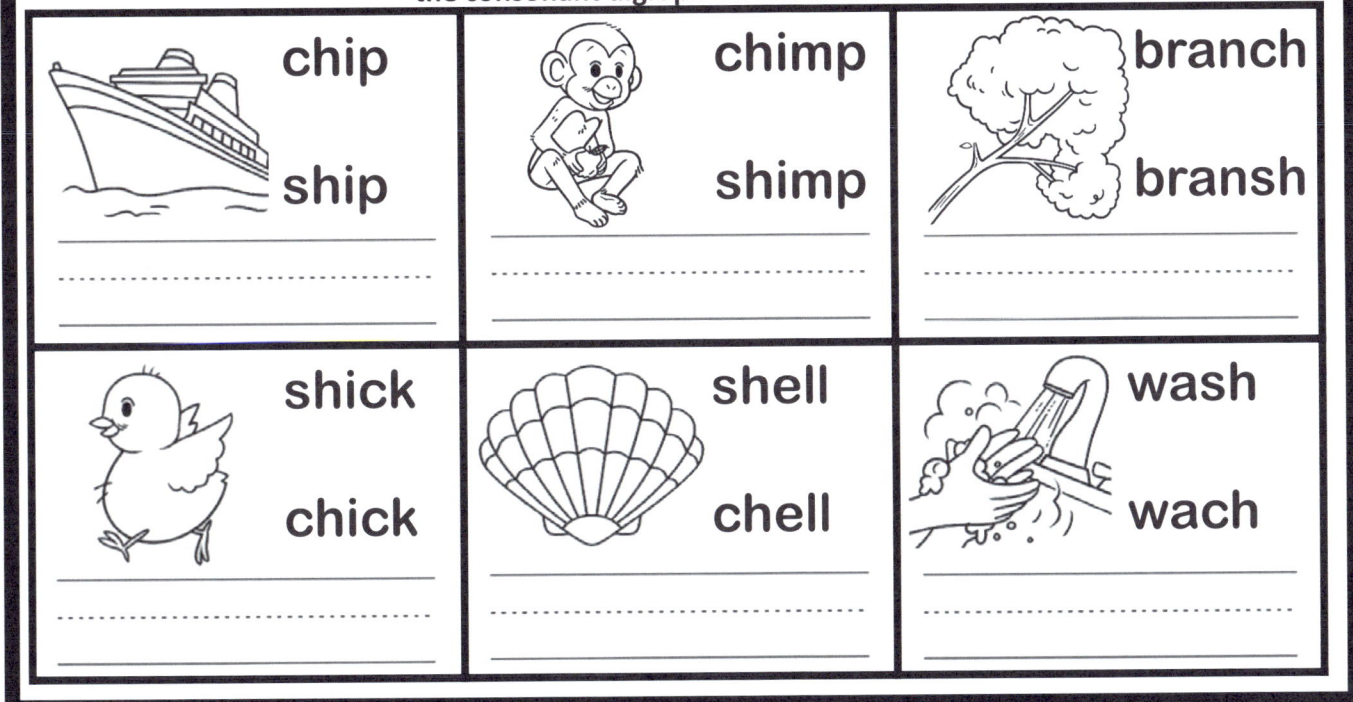

ship	chip / ship
monkey	chimp / shimp
branch	branch / bransh
chick	shick / chick
shell	shell / chell
wash	wash / wach

Grade 3 Phonics and Spelling Workbook — Created by Mrs. Indira Coleby-Demeritte

UNIT 23 Digraphs CH, SH, WH, TH — Page 143

WEDNESDAY — PHONICS PRACTICE

Look at each picture and say its name quietly to yourself. Write the consonant digraph sound (sh, ch, th, wh) that you hear.

[cherries] _____   [feather] _____   [peaches] _____

[sheep] _____   [think/math girl] _____   [wheel] _____

THURSDAY — PHONICS PRACTICE

Read the story and answer the questions.

The Three Kittens

Theo, Thelma, and Thad are three little kittens. They like to jump, play, and run through the kitchen. Theo is thirsty, so he stops to get a drink. Thelma and Thad keep jumping and playing. They think they are children, but they are just three little kittens.

1. What are the names of the three kittens?
   _____

2. Why does Theo stop to get a drink?
   _____

3. The kittens think they are what?
   _____

4. What is a synonym for <u>through</u>?
   Ⓐ around Ⓑ into and out of Ⓒ under Ⓓ top

Circle all of the <u>th</u> words in the story and then write the words in the box below.

Grade 3 Phonics and Spelling Workbook — Created by Mrs. Indira Coleby-Demeritte

UNIT 23 Digraphs CH, SH, WH, TH Page 144

ASSESSMENT

Date: _____   Score: _____

Directions: Read the word in the first column. Write the digraph in the second column. Fill in the bubble in the third column to show if the digraph is heard at the beginning, in the middle, or at the end of the word.

Digraphs			
ch	sh	th	wh

Word	Digraph	Position in Word		
		Beginning	Middle	End
1. cherry	ch	●	○	○
2. match		○	○	○
3. father		○	○	○
4. mouth		○	○	○
5. wash		○	○	○
6. lunch		○	○	○
7. sheep		○	○	○
8. teacher		○	○	○
9. whale		○	○	○
10. three		○	○	○
11. with		○	○	○
12. wheel		○	○	○

Grade 3 Phonics and Spelling Workbook   Created by Mrs. Indira Coleby-Demeritte

UNIT 23 Digraphs CH, SH, WH, TH

Page 145

MONDAY — SPELLING PRACTICE

Look at each picture and then write the spelling word that matches it.

TUESDAY — SPELLING PRACTICE

Use your spelling list to classify the words in the columns below.

Ch words	Sh words

Spelling Words

1. whisper
2. chin
3. shadow
4. thirteen
5. wheel
6. finish
7. ticklish
8. depth
9. whip
10. bench
11. fresh
12. worth
13. chance
14. watch
15. leash
16. which
17. check
18. sharp
19. thirsty
20. thermometer

Grade 3 Phonics and Spelling Workbook *Created by Mrs. Indira Coleby-Demeritte*

UNIT 23 Digraphs CH, SH, WH, TH — Page 146

WEDNESDAY — SPELLING PRACTICE

Circle the word spelled correctly in each column.

wisper / whisper / whispre / wispr	chanse / shance / chance / shans	finej / finishe / finish / finsh
thrtean / thirteen / thritene / thirtean	chadow / shadoe / shadoa / shadow	depth / death / dep / deth
wirth / worth / wurth / werth	ticklish / tklish / tiklij / ticklelish	weel / whele / weal / wheel

THURSDAY — SPELLING PRACTICE

Use your spelling list to classify the words in the columns below.

Th words	Wh words

Spelling Words

1. whisper
2. chin
3. shadow
4. thirteen
5. wheel
6. finish
7. ticklish
8. depth
9. whip
10. bench
11. fresh
12. worth
13. chance
14. watch
15. leash
16. which
17. check
18. sharp
19. thirsty
20. thermometer

UNIT 23 Digraphs CH, SH, WH, TH — Page 147

Practice the spelling of each word below by writing it in it's column.

whisper	chin	shadow	thirteen	wheel

finish	ticklish	depth	whip	bench

Grade 3 Phonics and Spelling Workbook — *Created by Mrs. Indira Coleby-Demeritte*

UNIT 23 Digraphs CH, SH, WH, TH — Page 148

Practice the spelling of each word below by writing it in it's column.

fresh	worth	chance	watch	leash

which	check	sharp	thirsty	thermometer

Grade 3 Phonics and Spelling Workbook — *Created by Mrs. Indira Coleby-Demeritte*

UNIT 24 Digraphs PH, GH, KN, GN — Page 149

MONDAY — PHONICS PRACTICE

Look at each picture and say its name to your self. Then color the consonant digraph sound you hear for each word.

telephone	ph / gn
gnome	gn / ph
gnat (fly)	gh / gn
knob	kn / ph
pharaoh	ph / kn
laugh	kn / gh

TUESDAY — PHONICS PRACTICE

Read the clues and use the words in the word box to fill in the blanks.

| gnaw | knock | gnat | knight | knife | knob |

1. This turns to open a door. _____
2. This can cut food items. _____
3. Mice do this to their food. _____
4. You make this sound on a door. _____
5. He works for a king. _____
6. This is a small bug. _____

UNIT 24 Digraphs PH, GH, KN, GN — Page 150

WEDNESDAY — PHONICS PRACTICE

Color all of the pictures that have the PH sound.

THURSDAY — PHONICS PRACTICE

Read the story and answer the questions.

Elephant Ride

Ralph and his nephew, Phil, went to the zoo. First, Phil wanted to see the amphibians. Next, Phil wanted to ride an elephant. Up, up, up, he climbed on top. The elephant took Phil for a ride. Ralph got out his phone and took a photo. Ralph is going to make a pamphlet of their day at the zoo.

1. Who went on a trip to the zoo?

2. What did Phil want to see first at the zoo?

3. What did Phil get to ride?

4. What is a synonym for pamphlet?
   A) draw B) ride C) small book D) paint

Circle all of the ph words in the story and then write the words in the box below.

Grade 3 Phonics and Spelling Workbook — Created by Mrs. Indira Coleby-Demeritte

UNIT 24 Digraphs PH, GH, KN, GN — Page 151

ASSESSMENT

Date: _____   Score: _____

Draw lines to match each word to its picture. There will be 2 words left over.

gnome

champagne

pharaoh

graph

microphone

knee

gnu

laugh

Grade 3 Phonics and Spelling Workbook   *Created by Mrs. Indira Coleby-Demeritte*

UNIT 24 Digraphs PH, GH, KN, GN — Page 152

MONDAY — SPELLING PRACTICE

Look at each picture and then write the spelling word that matches it.

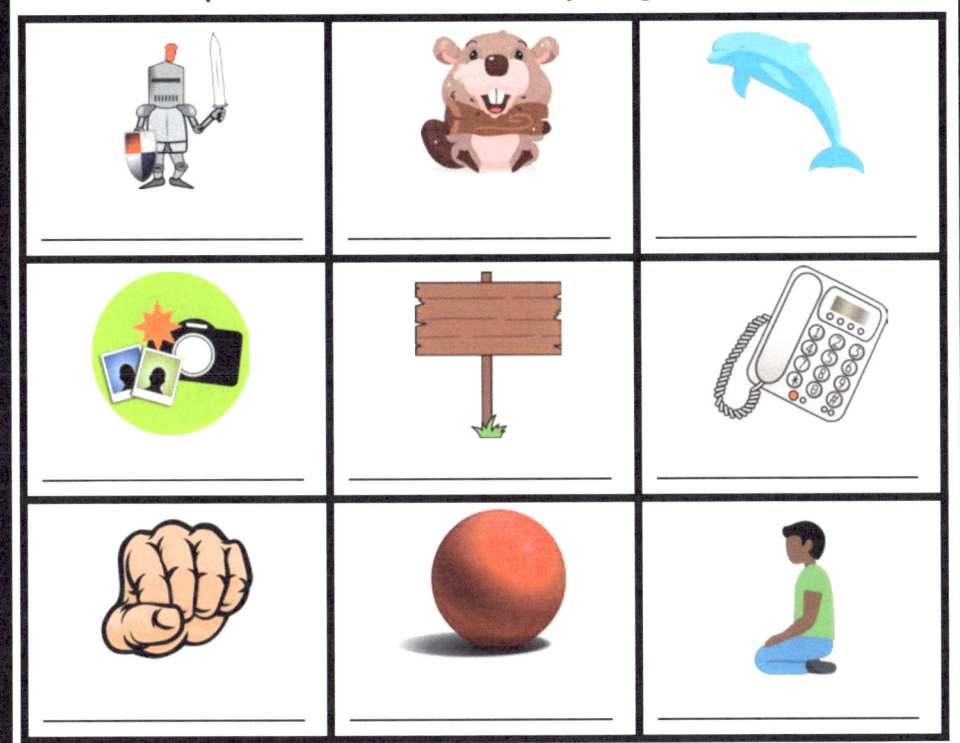

TUESDAY — SPELLING PRACTICE

Use your list words to classify the words below.

1 Syllable		2 Syllables	

3 Syllables		

Spelling Words

1. telephone
2. knowledge
3. sphere
4. enough
5. photograph
6. elephant
7. nephew
8. gnome
9. kneel
10. knight
11. dolphin
12. design
13. laugh
14. knuckle
15. cough
16. gnaw
17. sign
18. knife
19. tough
20. campaign

Grade 3 Phonics and Spelling Workbook — Created by Mrs. Indira Coleby-Demeritte

UNIT 24 Digraphs PH, GH, KN, GN — Page 153

WEDNESDAY — SPELLING PRACTICE

Use the word box to write an antonym for the words listed below.

nephew	knowledge	enough
kneel	tough	laugh

1. ignorance _____
2. more _____
3. stand _____
4. niece _____
5. cry _____
6. easy _____

THURSDAY — SPELLING PRACTICE

Look at the first letter of each word. Write the words in Alphabetical Order. The alphabet chart below will help you.

A B C D E F G H I J K L M N O P Q R S T U V W X Y Z

1. knuckle
2. dolphin
3. knife
4. campaign
5. gnome
6. gnaw

Spelling Words

1. telephone
2. knowledge
3. sphere
4. enough
5. photograph
6. elephant
7. nephew
8. gnome
9. kneel
10. knight
11. dolphin
12. design
13. laugh
14. knuckle
15. cough
16. gnaw
17. sign
18. knife
19. tough
20. campaign

Grade 3 Phonics and Spelling Workbook — Created by Mrs. Indira Coleby-Demeritte

UNIT 24 Digraphs PH, GH, KN, GN

Practice the spelling of each word below by writing it in it's column.

telephone	knowledge	sphere	enough	photograph

elephant	nephew	gnome	kneel	knight

Grade 3 Phonics and Spelling Workbook — *Created by Mrs. Indira Coleby-Demeritte*

UNIT 24 Digraphs PH, GH, KN, GN — Page 155

Practice the spelling of each word below by writing it in it's column.

dolphin	design	laugh	knuckle	cough

gnaw	sign	knife	tough	campaign

Grade 3 Phonics and Spelling Workbook *Created by Mrs. Indira Coleby-Demeritte*

| UNIT 25 Silent Letters WR & MB | Page 156 |

MONDAY — PHONICS PRACTICE

Look at each picture and say its name to yourself. Then color in the letter that you hear in the name.

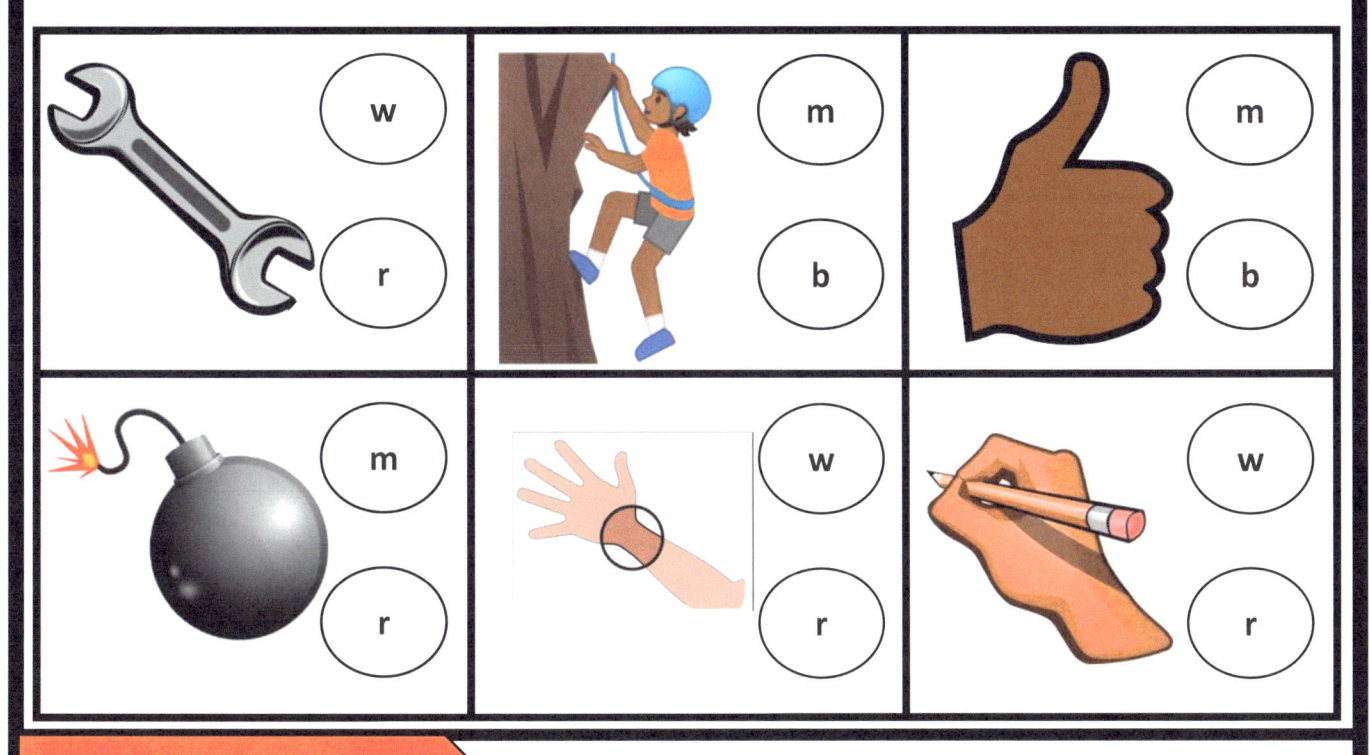

(wrench) w / r
(climber) m / b
(thumb) m / b
(bomb) m / r
(wrist) w / r
(write) w / r

TUESDAY — PHONICS PRACTICE

Read the clues and use the words in the word box to fill in the blanks.

| wrap | wren | wrong | write | wrench |

1. This word rhymes with then. It can fly _____
2. You do this with a pen. _____
3. You can fix things with this. _____
4. This is what you do to a gift. _____
5. This means "not right". _____

Grade 3 Phonics and Spelling Workbook   *Created by Mrs. Indira Coleby-Demeritte*

UNIT 25 Silent Letters WR & MB

WEDNESDAY — PHONICS PRACTICE

Look at the picture and word first in the row. Then circle the picture that has the same sound as the underlined letters.

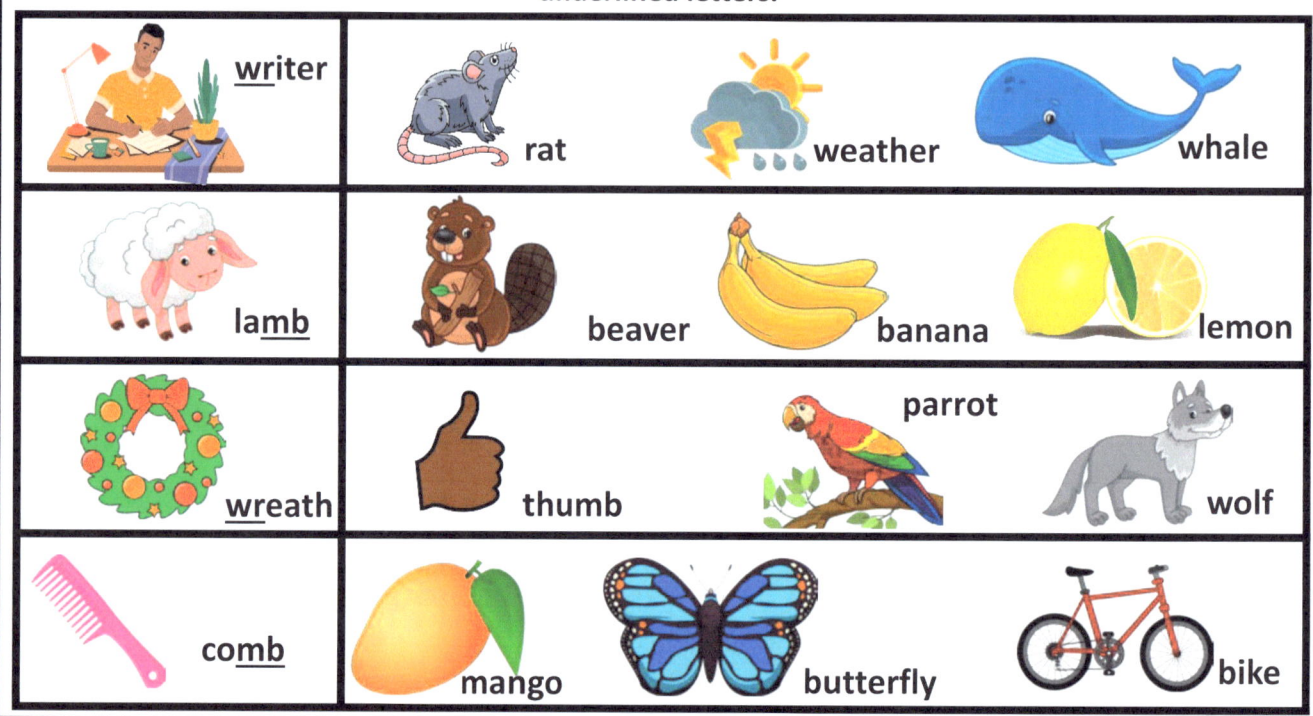

<u>wr</u>iter	rat	weather	whale
la<u>mb</u>	beaver	banana	lemon
<u>wr</u>eath	thumb	parrot	wolf
co<u>mb</u>	mango	butterfly	bike

THURSDAY — PHONICS PRACTICE

Read the story and answer the questions.

The Lamb and the Honeycomb

One day, I saw a lamb standing by a tree. There on a limb was a large honeycomb with a lot of bees around it. I knew not to climb the tree, because there was one bee the size of my thumb. The lamb and I got away from the bees and the honeycomb before we got stung.

1. What did I see standing by a tree?

2. What was on a limb of a tree?

3. One bee was the size of what?

4. What is a synonym for <u>limb</u>?
  Ⓐ flower Ⓑ branch Ⓒ trunk Ⓓ root

Circle all of the <u>mb</u> words in the story and then write the words in the box below.

Grade 3 Phonics and Spelling Workbook — Created by Mrs. Indira Coleby-Demeritte

UNIT 25 Silent Letters WR & MB   Page 158

ASSESSMENT

Date: _____   Score: _____

Use the word box to complete the sentences below.

climb	limb	comb	numb	crumb
plumber	jamb	thumb	tomb	lamb

1. The mouse found a _____ of bread on the floor.
2. The _____ fixed the clog in the sink.
3. Carson leaned against the door _____.
4. On the weekend, I will _____ the tree in the backyard.
5. On the third day Jesus was Resurrected from the _____.
6. The bird was singing while perched in the tree _____.
7. Mom made me _____ my hair before going to school.
8. The farmer made sure the _____ stayed near its mother sheep.
9. I crossed my legs too long so my feet began to feel _____.
10. My sister did a great job, so I pointed my _____ up in the air.

Grade 3 Phonics and Spelling Workbook   *Created by Mrs. Indira Coleby-Demeritte*

UNIT 25 Silent Letters WR & MB Page 159

MONDAY — SPELLING PRACTICE

Look at each picture and then write the spelling word that matches it.

TUESDAY — SPELLING PRACTICE

Look at the first letter of each word. Write the words in Alphabetical Order. The alphabet chart below will help you.

A B C D **E** F G H **I** J K L M N **O** P Q R S T **U** V W X Y Z

1. wrestle
2. wrist
3. wrench
4. wreck
5. wrinkle
6. wreath

Spelling Words

1. lamb
2. comb
3. crumb
4. climb
5. limb
6. thumb
7. tomb
8. numb
9. bomb
10. plumber
11. write
12. wrap
13. wrong
14. wrestle
15. wrist
16. wren
17. wrench
18. wrinkle
19. wreath
20. wreck

Grade 3 Phonics and Spelling Workbook   *Created by Mrs. Indira Coleby-Demeritte*

UNIT 25 Silent Letters WR & MB

Page 160

WEDNESDAY — SPELLING PRACTICE

Use the word box to write a rhyming word for the words listed below.

comb	write	wreck
plumber	wrench	crumb

1. dumber _____
2. deck _____
3. boom _____
4. bench _____
5. bright _____
6. plum _____

THURSDAY — SPELLING PRACTICE

Circle the word spelled correctly in each column.

when wren ren wen	numb num nub knumb	lim lib limb libm
rinkle rinkl wrinkel wrinkle	rappe wrap rapp wrape	thumb thum thub tubm
restle westl restel wrestle	bomb boom bobm mbom	krum crumb krumb crubm

Spelling Words

1. lamb
2. comb
3. crumb
4. climb
5. limb
6. thumb
7. tomb
8. numb
9. bomb
10. plumber
11. write
12. wrap
13. wrong
14. wrestle
15. wrist
16. wren
17. wrench
18. wrinkle
19. wreath
20. wreck

Grade 3 Phonics and Spelling Workbook Created by Mrs. Indira Coleby-Demeritte

UNIT 25 Silent Letters WR & MB — Page 161

Practice the spelling of each word below by writing it in it's column.

lamb	comb	crumb	climb	limb

thumb	tomb	numb	bomb	plumber

UNIT 25 Silent Letters WR & MB — Page 162

Practice the spelling of each word below by writing it in it's column.

write	wrap	wrong	wrestle	wrist

wren	wrench	wrinkle	wreath	wreck

Made in the USA
Columbia, SC
05 July 2024